Mindfulness *for* Unravelling Anxiety

Mindfulness *for* Unravelling Anxiety

Finding Calm & Clarity in Uncertain Times

Richard Gilpin

Leaping Hare Press

This edition published in the UK and North America in 2018 by

Leaping Hare Press

An imprint of The Quarto Group
The Old Brewery, 6 Blundell Street
London N7 9BH, United Kingdom
T (0)20 7700 6700
www.QuartoKnows.com

First published in the UK in 2016

Text copyright © 2016 Richard Gilpin
Design and layout copyright © 2017 Quarto Publishing plc

British Library Cataloguing-in-Publication Data
A catalogue record for this book is available from the British Library

ISBN: 978-1-78240-318-0

This book was conceived, designed and produced by

Leaping Hare Press

58 West Street, Brighton BN1 2RA, United Kingdom

Publisher SUSAN KELLY
Creative Director MICHAEL WHITEHEAD
Editorial Director TOM KITCH
Commissioning Editor MONICA PERDONI
Art Director WAYNE BLADES
Project Editor JOANNA BENTLEY
Editor JENNI DAVIS
Designer GINNY ZEAL
Illustrator MELVYN EVANS

Printed in China

5 7 9 10 8 6

CONTENTS

INTRODUCTION

Everybody gets anxious. Anxiety principally
concerns our relationship with the future — the
anticipation of which can provoke disquiet and even
dread. The future only exists in the mind, so it is to our
mental world that we must turn if we are to alleviate
anxiety. This is where our wonderful capacity to be
mindful comes in. Mindfulness is principally about our
relationship with the present — a 'being with' what is
happening now, in all its vividness and perplexity.
Where mindfulness meets anxiety, then, is in the
obscure interzone between 'now' and 'later'.

START WHERE YOU ARE

◆

To mindfully untangle from anxiety is a journey of self-discovery. It involves learning to be intimate with anxiety and finding a release from its grip through the power of affectionate awareness and the practice of skilful responding.

THIS BOOK OFFERS SOME TRIED AND TESTED ways, ancient and modern, for doing just that. It is part road map, part toolkit, part inspiration for the journey. It is not a substitute for the journey itself, which only you can make. Such an inner journey differs from an outer one in one crucial aspect: the path and the destination are not separate. The journey's means and ends are fused in a dynamic harmony. We drop our driven pursuit of goals and simply start where we are. Every step *is* the achievement. Working mindfully with anxiety involves tuning in to the immediacy of life – what may be so obvious that we overlook it. The materials we use are the raw data from which we make sense of our world – thoughts, feelings, sensory stimuli… everything, in fact, we call 'reality'.

The Nature of Anxiety

As a therapist who works regularly with anxiety sufferers, I have become familiar with its distinctive features – its foreboding presence in a person's life, its unsettling and debilitating effects, its wisplike occupancy of a mind whose thoughts, in contrast, feel like wrecking balls. Anxiety comes in many forms, but what commonly strikes me about it is its ensnaring quality – the way it throws people 'onto the back foot', leaving them disorientated and doubtful. Anxiety robs us of our natural spontaneity and our chance to flourish in the world.

I also know about anxiety through personal experience – its visceral grip and tremorous energy, the jagged thinking and vacillating behaviour I fall into, the hellish claustrophobia that comes from feeling suffocated by the future. Because of its bewildering impact, I find anxiety a tricky state to pin down. It can feel so 'unreal' at the time that it is difficult to clearly recall afterwards – as if it happened in another world or to someone else. It can, therefore, be a challenging state to be curious about. But when I do get curious, I find this is time and energy well spent.

Curiosity is an essential ingredient for good mindfulness practice. To mindfully investigate anxiety is to turn towards it – to see and feel it intimately. With clear seeing comes understanding. To witness, at first hand, how anxiety conjures itself into existence is to reveal something of its true nature. When I realize the stories my anxious mind tells me about the future are just that – stories – they lose their hold over me. If my anxious thoughts had any validity, I would have wound up, long ago, either dead or destitute. How sweet it is to break free from the fabrications of my deluded mind!

The Reality Check of Mindfulness

Showing a friendly interest in anxiety is, of course, counter-intuitive since it is usually something we try to avoid. Here lies the reality check of mindfulness, which invites us to acknowledge the *fact* of anxiety – its natural place in the scheme of human experience – and to witness how the urge to avoid it is not only unrealistic but can also make matters worse by feeding deep-seated tendencies that maintain subjective distress. Mindfulness practice involves a forthright 'knowing' of anxiety – not to get rid of it, or even change it, but to embrace it and let it be. When we learn to let things be, we learn to let them go.

Mindfulness practice involves a forthright 'knowing' of anxiety

Learn to let go of anxiety – *really* let go – and it ceases to be a problem. What was once an interminable blight on one's life is transformed into empty bursts of sensations and fantastical parades of mental hype dissolving in space. This is possible through the practice of mindfulness – the clear, receptive, even-minded awareness of what is happening as it is happening. Under the steady, non-discriminating flood-lights of mindful awareness, anxiety is exposed for what it is. Its illusions of permanency and substantiality are blown apart. It fizzles and fades like a Halloween sparkler. A new relationship with it becomes possible – one where resistance is replaced by acceptance and anguish turns to ease.

VANISHING POINT

For me, writing this book has been an immersion in its subject mat-
ter. I remember the first time anxiety, mindfulness and this book all
converged at a single point in time. It was a month before I started
writing, during a day-long mindfulness retreat.

I HAD BEEN ENJOYING A RESTFUL MORNING of meditation, sharing the silence with a congenial group of people. But, as the retreat progressed, I had become aware of indistinct tensions gathering inside me – a fuzzy tightness in my mind and elusive thoughts that seemed to chisel in the background. Physically, too, I felt ill at ease.

By the afternoon, my edginess had intensified. During a period of walking meditation, I became so disturbed that I could ignore the feelings no longer. Objectively, life seemed good – it was Saturday afternoon, I was doing what I wanted and, outwardly at least, all was serene. The way I felt made no sense. Then I recalled what I was supposed to be doing – prac-tising mindfulness – and noted the ideal circumstances for exploring what was happening within me. So I dropped all my pondering, stood absolutely still, grounded myself through my body, opened up to my feelings and did absolutely noth-ing. In the stillness and spaciousness of the moments that followed there arose, for the first time, a clear recognition that I was deeply anxious at the prospect of writing this book.

A Dawning Moment

Up until then, I'd *thought* I was excited about it! I had spent months mulling over the book's content, making notes and looking forward to a new creative project. But soon it would be time to get down to the hard graft of writing. All the irksome juggling of book work, day job and other responsibilities was imminent. These stressors had been hovering on the horizons of my mind like storm clouds. I'd been playing host to them without even realizing it.

My mind had been doing its 'early warning' routine, hence all my uneasiness. Becoming aware of what was bothering me *and* 'getting real' about the future left me free to mentally park the whole lot and appreciate some mindful walking.

FINDING YOUR OWN WAY

Any book on mindfulness can only be a signpost and not the location itself. Mindfulness emphasizes the authority of experience, not of theory or doctrine. The pages ahead are an invitation to experiment with how you might live more mindfully and less anxiously.

READING BOOKS, HOWEVER, IS NOT ENOUGH. Practice is required. 'Practice', in mindfulness terms, comprises enquiry, reflection, meditation and action. To aid your efforts, threaded through the book are several traditional meditations and reflective exercises.

To practise the meditations, it is advisable to first record the instructions onto an audio device (leaving a gap of two or three minutes between each instruction) and then play the recording as you meditate. If you have no recording device, ask someone to read the instructions to you. The reflective exercises that indicate using a pen and paper do so for good reason – attempting to do them in your head will undermine your objectivity and induce confusion. Consistent, daily practice, particularly of the meditative variety, *will* deliver positive change to your life – possibly in ways you never imagined. Mindfulness has a habit of conferring unexpected gifts.

One Step at a Time

Mindfulness is a gradual training. We begin in its shallower waters and progressively go deeper. This book approaches its subject matter in kind. The first chapter is all about getting to know anxiety – its nature, function and impact. The second chapter explores practical steps for dealing with it through mindful enquiry and reflection. The third chapter maps the territory of mindfulness practice in depth. The final chapter delves into the implications of centralizing mindfulness in one's life. That said, every chapter is complete in itself so, if you prefer, you can dip into this book anywhere. On the path of mindfulness we have to find our own way, so how you apply any knowledge you gain from this book is all that matters. I hope it inspires you to take your practice further.

CHAPTER ONE

STATES OF EMERGENCY

*To be anxious is to be alive. Human beings
face persistent unknowns and innumerable dangers.
Anxiety-free worlds are the stuff of mythical pasts and
mythical futures. In our efforts to preserve ourselves amid
unpredictability, we are prone to vexation, doubt and fear.
This is understandable but it does not mean we have to
live in anguish. Exploring the terrain of anxiety helps us
get better acquainted with the bare elements of our
existence — physical sensations, emotions, thoughts and
actions. This marks the beginning of a wise
relationship with an essential aspect
of the human condition.*

THERE MAY BE TROUBLE AHEAD

◆

Life abounds with possibilities. From this rich potential spring the many wonders that are humanity's birthright. But such potential has a flip side, for unwritten futures also carry with them the risk of unwelcome outcomes. It is within the gap between our sense of a present and our sense of a future — deep in the mystifying flux of what is actual and what is conceivable — that we find the origins of anxiety.

THE WORD 'ANXIETY' DERIVES FROM the Latin *anxietas*, meaning 'troubled in mind', which tells us something of the essential nature of this common experience: its tone is disturbing, its footing is mental. A deeper linguistic root is the Greek *angho*, which translates as 'to squeeze'. This conveys the feeling of an energy force that exerts pressure and constriction. From this sense of being gripped painfully, *angho* evolved to mean being 'burdened' or 'weighed down with trouble'.

To be anxious, then, is to find oneself in the stranglehold of mental uneasiness. The mind becomes possessed by vague ideas of things being, or going, wrong. It shrink-wraps life

◆

The beginning of wisdom
is to call things by their right names.

CONFUCIUS
551–479 BCE, PHILOSOPHER

◆

into something that looks and tastes unsavoury. We feel cramped and uptight as a result. The tendency, then, is to behave erratically – to balk, blink, freeze or falter.

Anxiety blurs the boundaries between the real and the imagined. We can get anxious about almost anything: work, ageing, illness, insolvency, our loved ones, environmental catastrophe, nuclear war. The possibility of any one of a multitude of threats, occurring when we least expect it, is readily available to the incredible human mind, which can conjure up any eventuality (and frequently does). Sprinkle in the chance of desired outcomes going unrealized, add the prospect of anything currently going well not lasting, and we succeed in reducing life to an ominous state of affairs. Ouch.

The Fear Factor

Anxiety is part of the territory for any self-aware creature capable of abstract thought. We know this world can be inhospitable and even hostile. We know things can go wrong. When we anticipate impending situations for which we feel ill-equipped, it is natural to go on the alert. This is an attempt to exert control. Anxiety can be understood as an adaptive response to an indefinite number of unfavourable possibilities. It has a survival function – organisms that get anxious when facing potential threats are more likely to carry on living and reproducing. From this perspective, anxiety appears to be a close cousin of another basic human experience: fear.

Fear is our alarm response to danger. It is the appraisal of a perilous event or object that is in our vicinity – either physically near or temporally near. It is marked by physiological arousal (changes in breathing and heart rate) and bodily action (tackling or avoiding the danger). Fear is specific: it is about a *particular* object or event we perceive to be threatening. When we are fearful, we are focusing on our *proximity* to what frightens us.

Anxiety requires no specific object or event from which to develop itself. It requires no proximity to threats actual or imagined. Sources of anxiety are often unclear, yet they linger as tensions in the body and loom like ghosts in the mind. At such times, haunted by the unpredictable and uncontrollable aspects of our existence, the difference between fear and anxiety might seem rather academic.

Going Off Piste

Once, lost in the Himalayas, I had a memorable encounter with fear and anxiety. I had gone for an afternoon walk with two friends up a mountain. We had strayed from the main path and got disorientated. In our hunt for a way down, we found only precipitous drops. We were forced further up the mountain, seeking any sign of any path. Then the sun began to drop. In the dimming light, it became too dangerous to continue searching for a track. Ill-equipped for a night at altitude in sub-zero temperatures, we paused to fortify ourselves with some bananas and consider our situation.

When I heard the concern in my friends' voices, the icy chill of fear bit into me. My chest felt like a lead weight. My throat was tight and dry. My mind flooded with the real possibilities of being lost for days, getting attacked by wild animals or freezing to death. Such was the hijacking power of my fears, I was struck dumb for some time, unable to contribute to a very practical discussion my friends were having about what to do next.

Peak Moments

After some minutes, the physical tension eased and my breathing softened. I found my voice enough to agree to a bold plan of scaling several hundred metres upwards to a tree-lined hilltop, which appeared to be our best chance of finding shelter for the night. On that crown of dry earth canopied by two pine trees, we found enough twigs, branches and, crucially, an old tree stump to maintain a fire that burned until dawn.

Between us, we had snack food, some mint leaf, two mugs, a stainless steel bowl and Swiss Army knives. We spent the night tending the fire, boiling down snow to make mint tea and huddling together, sometimes telling stories, often falling silent, humbled by the immensity of the landscape. Perched on rock, enclosed by snow, sustained by fire, nourished by air (and tea), it was a profoundly elemental experience. The morning sun rising over a line of Himalayan snow peaks is one of the most awe-inspiring things I have ever seen.

My fear had long dissolved, but my anxiety loitered throughout the night and into my descent from the mountain the next morning. I kept brooding on the fragility of my situation and the endless potential for dangers to arise. I felt butterflies in my stomach every time I fell captive to the currents of unnerving 'What if?' thoughts trickling through my head. My mind seemed drawn like a magnet to jumbles of undefined calamities. My body pulsed as if on perpetual 'amber alert'. I only eased up once off the mountain.

It is the nature of anxiety to hover indeterminately, to take up headspace, induce tension, and edge out the joys of life's adventures. It is the nature of humans to get anxious. But being anxious does not have to be distressing or arduous.

EXCITEMENT WITHOUT OXYGEN

◆

Many people associate anxiety with unpleasant bodily symptoms such as tension and impaired breathing and, therefore, try to avoid it. Perhaps you are reading this book because you want to find ways to stop feeling anxious or reduce its occurrence in your life.

THIS IS UNDERSTANDABLE but takes no account of the kind of anxious feelings you can have for desirable outcomes. The breathless anticipation for something to turn out the way you want is closely related to anxiety. The more you explore anxiety, the more nuances you find.

Anxiety is the gap between the *now* and the *then*.

FRITZ PERLS
1893–1970, PSYCHOTHERAPIST[1]

As with fear, anxiety has a close cousin in excitement. Excitement is aligned to our primal urge to live. It is our nature to seek out what we need in order to survive, grow and prosper. Excitement is the mobilizing of our energy to achieve this. Excitement leads to action. Through action, we meet our needs. Through meeting our needs we live more fully. Without excitement, we would be catatonic.

Life, Interrupted

Excitement is the spontaneous leap into the next moment of our life. But what if this flow forwards gets interrupted? What if we resist, hold back and get stuck in the tension between our experience of 'now' and our perception of 'later'? What if we lose our nerve and don't dare to take the next leap? In this hiatus we find the enduring human propensity for anxiety.

This is the subtle rendering of anxiety put forward by the eminent psychotherapist Fritz Perls.[2] Anxiety, said Perls, is the conflict between our natural excitement and our tendency for self-control. This conflict interferes with our most vital function: breathing. Suspended in the uncertainty between 'now' and 'later', we attempt to be 'calm and collected'. In so doing,

we block our excitement and deprive ourselves of our most essential need: the healthy flow of breath. In the visceral collision of our wants, needs, doubts and fears, we experience excitement without oxygen.

HUMAN COMPOSITIONS

Throughout the centuries, anxiety has variously been categorized as a psychological problem, a physiological syndrome, a philosophical enquiry and an existential predicament. Depending on where you stand and how you look at it, anxiety presents a different face.

THE STUDY OF ANXIETY IN MODERN TIMES tends towards the psychological, viewing it as a distressing emotion with complex connections to personality and environmental factors. Seen through this lens, anxiety is about negative anticipation: the tendency to focus on impending situations with a perceived inability to cope. It is about threat — of overwhelm, over-stimulation and unmanageable demands, all flavoured with large doses of urgency and doubt.

The recipe is slightly different for every person. It depends on your current circumstances *and* how you manage stress. 'Trait anxiety', which is related to personality, is the relatively stable, ongoing level of anxiety a person has regardless of the situation. People with higher levels of trait anxiety get stressed more easily. 'State anxiety' is a more transitory form of anxiety and is related to particular situations. It is characterized by heightened emotion and often affects performance. The distinction between trait and state anxiety has endured since ancient Roman times, as has the understanding that people with higher levels of trait anxiety experience more intense state anxiety in a broader range of situations.

A Bundle of Nerves

Ask most people about their anxiety and they recollect how it feels. Trembling, shaking, dizziness, breathlessness, sweating, restlessness, nausea, tension and chest pain are common symptoms. From hot heads to cold feet, feeling 'unreal' to feeling 'too real', anxiety is a memorable experience. It's meant to be. It's the body's way of saying that something is up.

Anxiety has been a constant backdrop to human history. As a species, we evolved amid life-threatening dangers, so anxiety is part of our heritage. To be wary and to worry are survival instincts. Unlike our prehistoric ancestry, most of us today do not contend daily with predators, starvation and other grave threats. But the basic programming to deal with such eventualities remains embedded within us. Our evolutionary history has determined that our minds filter reality much like our mammalian, primate and human forebears, who were obliged to repeatedly wonder: 'Can I eat that or will that eat me?' Their default assumption was that something was dangerous until proven otherwise.

Naked Apes

In many ways, the human species has not changed much through the ages. One thing that has changed, though, is our knowledge of biology and neurophysiology. We now know what is happening within our bodies when we get anxious.

In the limbic system of your brain are two structures called amygdalae, which form the epicentre of a primitive alarm system. When you perceive a threat, the amygdalae pulse warnings to different parts of the brain, which initiate a bio-chemical chain reaction that sends your entire organism into a state of high nervous arousal. It's like a firework going off in your head and exploding in the centre of your body.

You are now in threat mode, primed for danger. Rational thinking goes 'offline'. In seconds, your body is awash with stress hormones. Your rate of breathing increases. Your senses sharpen. Impulses quicken. Muscles and limbs mobilize in readiness for action. Like your ancient forebears, you are ready to take on a woolly mammoth.

Perceiving a threat, we become the vigilant hunter and/or hunted in a second. Faced with uncertainty, we incline towards caution and restraint. We are sensitive creatures who take a 'better safe than sorry' approach to life. It is no wonder, then, that our minds can act in one moment like an arsonist, inflaming situations with abandon, and in the next like a pan-icking health and safety officer, mindlessly ringing alarm bells in a desperate attempt to keep control.

Creature Comforts

Our hereditary instincts can feel confusing, given how life is for us today – top of the food chain and calling all the shots. With flesh-eating predators absent, we are more likely to battle our own emotions instead. In order to not feel threatened, anxious or panicky, we may employ the same primitive programming designed for dealing with external threats: control and avoidance. Control is about forcibly changing or getting rid of the thing(s) we perceive to be dangerous. Avoidance concerns removing ourselves from the situation, or not entering it in the first place. In any physically life-threatening circumstances, both strategies are ideal. Our ancient ancestors would attest to it.

EXERCISE

WHAT'S THE WEATHER LIKE?

❋

Weather terms are a rich source of language for describing emotions. Examples are feeling calm, unsettled, dull, bright and turbulent. Finding a word to describe the 'weather inside' lends a degree of objectivity to your experience. When you notice that you are anxious, first let yourself feel it in your body, then find a weather term that fits with the feeling. Does your anxiety feel like a storm, a tremor, a squall, a wildfire, a sinkhole, a lightning strike, a tornado…? As with any good weather report, stick to the headlines and remember to provide yourself with regular updates.

But what if your life is not in danger? What if the 'threat' is just an idea in your mind? Here, your efforts to restore a state of comfort and ease break down. Control and avoidance prevent further exploration of the 'danger'. The nature of the 'danger' remains scarily ill-defined. Control and avoidance also cause mental conflict if you try to control or avoid ideas in your mind (which you will, if these are what are troubling you). The overall result tends to be more, not less, emotional distress. In the absence of a direct threat to your life, control and avoidance offer little more than lush turf for a self-generating cycle of anxiety.

If we keep using the same tools, we're going to get the same results. This is true for control and avoidance, both of which kill curiosity. Without curiosity, we realize nothing new. Perhaps this is why, despite relative comfort and security for many of us, we live in a so-called 'age of anxiety' where recorded levels of anxiety are at a peak.

More than ever in human history, growing numbers of humans live safer, healthier and longer lives. We have food, first-aid kits and insurance policies. It is true that greater freedom and prosperity have brought new problems of social identity and connection – but why are so many of us so anxious? To find out, we need to discover what is happening *inside*. How we perceive our world, ourselves and each other are huge markers for how we will feel. The first, small step to unravelling anxiety is to go inwards and get curious.

EXERCISE

DECONSTRUCTING ANXIETY

✳

Reflect on your personal experiences of anxiety. What comes to mind? Feelings? Images? Places? People? Memories? Actions? Sensations? With a pen and paper, make a note of everything, no matter how random.

Now arrange what you've written into the different domains below. More material will come to mind as you do this.

• **Triggers:** When are the times you are most likely to get anxious? What things, places or people trigger anxiety? What might you see, hear, touch, taste, smell and think that trigger anxiety?

• **Bodily sensations:** What do you feel in your body when you are anxious? Do you feel changes in temperature, breathing, tension, alertness? Where in your body? Write down everything you feel, from the most obvious to the most subtle.

• **Thoughts:** What runs through your mind during anxious times? Are there specific thoughts like 'I'm in danger', 'I won't cope', 'The worst will happen'? Are there mental images? Is there an internal, running commentary about what you are thinking and how you are feeling?

• **Behaviours:** What do you do when you feel anxious? Leave situations? Stay at home? Keep close to others? Move away from others? Who, what and where do you avoid? What do you do more (or less) of? On what do you focus your attention?

Now that you have deconstructed your anxiety, what do you notice about it? Are some domains more discernible than others? What connections are there between different domains? Does anxiety seem less like one 'thing' and more like an arrangement of related factors?

FRONTLOADING THE FUTURE

◆

One stormy evening, I stood in my hallway looking skyward through a glass-panelled roof at some high guttering that had come loose. It was shaking and swaying and cascading streams of water onto the roof. I thought it might collapse and crack the glass. There was nothing I could do. I kept wandering off and coming back to take another look. It was a futile way to spend three hours of my life.

UP AND DOWN THE HALLWAY I shuffled, peering into the cloudburst above, eyeballing that gutter. When I wasn't visually focusing on it, I was somewhere else in the house thinking about it. I did not have the knowledge or ability to fix it myself. Feeling helpless and uptight, I spent an entire evening playing out scenes in my mind of tumbling drains, smashing glass and flooded hallways. My first practical action was calling a builder the next morning to come and examine the guttering. My behaviour that evening effected no change and amounted to just one thing: worrying.

Like many people, I have been in tough spots in my life. I have faced physical threats, painful challenges of injury and illness, and suffered numerous losses. Several times I have brushed with death. Myself and loved ones have been bruised by calamity and misfortune. But when life is sweet, save for a rainstorm, I can happily spend hours worrying myself stupid about the most tedious of things, like wobbly gutters.

Our worst misfortunes never happen,

and most miseries lie in anticipation.

HONORÉ DE BALZAC
1799–1850, NOVELIST

Fictional Productions

Mine is a mundane example that highlights a characteristic of the capricious human mind. Faced with the potential for an unwelcome event taking place, the mind, left unchecked, tends to fixate on it. It constructs a mental representation of the object of concern and focuses recurrently on it (often to the exclusion of everything else). In this state of preoccupation, the mind becomes so engrossed with its object that it loses a clear sense of present circumstances – what is *actually* happening. The mind, effectively, loses its bearings. The result can be hours spent wandering up and down hallways in the rain, vexed and vacillating, accomplishing nothing.

You probably know this experience for yourself. The ability to harvest disaster from thin air is, after all, part of our mental heritage. Your mind gets captivated by some kind of negative prophecy. It hijacks your powers of concentration and shuts down your capacity to take effective action. Seduced into a virtual future of misfortune, you waste hours embroiled in these fantasies until you feel exhausted. This is something normal human minds do. They're good at it. It's a problem.

Life As Disaster Movie

Worrying is repetitive, negative, future-focused thinking. It is the double-bind of being unable to resolve something in the mind while feeling compelled to keep focusing on it. In 'worry mode', we are preoccupied by chains of catastrophic thinking. These thought-chains are unstable – they billow outwards like nuclear mushroom clouds, generating more and more unfavourable scenarios. This is the mind making its own disaster movies. Why does it do that? Because humans are born problem-solvers engaged in an ongoing relationship with an uncertain future, but we get confused between doing something practical to address an issue (problem-solving) and thinking negatively about it over and over again (worrying). The latter is rooted in a flawed relationship with the future. It can also be a compulsive behaviour: you prod at the same stale, old worries and they nag right back at you.

In my work as a therapist, most clients who present with anxiety issues also indicate strong tendencies to worry. One client described how he was 'tortured by future possibilities', another how she 'borrowed problems from tomorrow', another how he would wake up each morning and 'mentally pull a lever so that a load of worry bricks come tumbling down on my head'. Such remarks all point to a tendency of paralysing present-moment experience by ladening the mind with the future. It's no surprise that the old English word *wrygan*, from which 'worry' derives, means 'to strangle'.

EXERCISE

HOW CLEAN IS YOUR CRYSTAL BALL?

✳

Write down an example of something you are worrying about, such as an impending event. Next, write down what you are telling yourself will happen in the future that relates to this worry. Now distil this into a specific prediction: what *exactly* will happen? When *exactly*? Where *exactly*? How *exactly*? Write down every detail. Avoid generalities. Your prediction should be so clear that other people besides you will know if this event occurs or not. Now you should have a precise description of a specific event. This is what your mind is saying the future holds. Are you sure? Really?

Lost in the Mist

Giving credence to our worries precipitates states of free-floating anxiety. This kind of anxiety tends to be self-generating because when we don't know what we're anxious about, we get anxious about getting anxious.

Worrying is the fuel for this vicious cycle. When we worry, such is the extent of our departure from reality into the virtual world of the mind that we temporarily cut off from our emotional experience. Upon 'return', we come into contact with our emotions, expressed through the body, only now we've lost the link between what we feel (anxiety) and what gave rise to it in the first place (worry). This triggers more urges to worry and maintains anxious arousal.

There is no point in worrying about worrying. It just leads to more… you know what. Trust that the key to a worry-free life *is* possible. It primarily comes through understanding more about how your mind works. Mindfulness practice provides this understanding and leads towards that kind of life.

BACK TO BEGINNINGS

Humans have always got anxious and we always will. We don't have to make this a problem. How we relate to our anxiety and how we apply our knowledge of it are the constructive objects of enquiry. Putting the focus here offers a different perspective on how to handle our troubled hearts and minds.

READ UP ON ANXIETY and you quickly discover its abiding presence in the history of humankind. Some of the earliest records of people expressing themselves are Paleolithic cave paintings, depicting menageries of ancient beasts prowling, stampeding and fighting. Others depict hunting scenes. The essential message conveyed could be: 'I am hunter. I am hunted. Life is dangerous. I can paint. Welcome to my world.'

Fast-forward to today and anxious humans abound. Is it any wonder? News headlines bombard us with stories of war, pandemics, poverty and destruction. We anguish over our children, security, money, health, sex appeal and how we stack up against our peers and neighbours.

Entire industries are built on the human propensity to get anxious. Marketing campaigns spread fear of germs we never knew existed and covertly hammer our morale for having the wrong car, hair or shoes. A toxic combination of real threats and manufactured fears has implanted anxiety into our lives like never before. To deal with the emotional debris, we turn to medication, entertainment and insurance companies.

New World Disorders

Anxiety viewed as an 'illness' is a more recent phenomenon. It was not until the nineteenth century that mental troubles were viewed as diseases. Prior to that, they were linked to character traits or individual failings. The ancient Greeks explained anxiety as 'the expectation of evil'[3] (where the 'evil' could be anything from social disgrace to death). Robert Burton's *The Anatomy of Melancholy* (1621), described anxiety as an innate human affliction, one strongly linked to melancholia (a forerunner for the term 'depression').[4]

The influential work of Sigmund Freud (1856–1939) was the first to isolate anxiety from other psychological problems and to classify its different manifestations. That said, the contemporary classification of 'anxiety disorders' (see box on page 35) has shifted since Freud's time. Their definitions and the way they are categorized remain fluid. They are notoriously controversial among psychotherapists. Some swear by them, others consider them stumbling blocks.

One thing is for sure – diagnoses are too arbitrary and simplistic to yield anything more than a signpost to someone's suffering. Diagnostic tools used by professionals cannot be truly objective due to the complexity of factors (environmental, social, biological, psychological) that contribute to mental health. At their worst, diagnoses of anxiety reduce people to sets of abnormal-sounding symptoms and indirectly feed a profiteering pharmaceutical industry. At their best, diagnoses are a nod to the multifaceted nature of anxiety. By distinguishing between clusters of common symptoms, they can be a skilful means to track how an individual's distress deviates from more general human dis-ease.

Ticket to Ride

A good metaphor for what connects all anxiety disorders is a fairground carousel consisting of many horses. Each horse represents a distinct thought, type of behaviour or bias of attention. A particular grouping of horses represents the unique constellation of factors that makes up one disorder. Some horses are shared among different disorders; others are specific to one disorder. What do not change, however, are the central hub of the carousel and the overall ride, which is always round and round. The hub and the ride – the basic mechanisms of all anxiety – are common to every disorder and the only essential things to know about. The next chapter explores these in more detail.

Classifications of Anxiety

GENERALIZED ANXIETY DISORDER: Marked tendency to persistently worry about many things, accompanied by physical symptoms of anxiety.

SPECIFIC PHOBIA: Fear of a particular object, event or situation.

PANIC DISORDER: Persistent fear of one's own physiological threat reactions.

AGORAPHOBIA: Avoidance of venturing out for fear of having a panic attack.

SOCIAL ANXIETY DISORDER: Fear of being judged, ridiculed or humiliated in front of other people (possibly through displaying visible signs of anxiety).

HEALTH ANXIETY *: Marked concern for one's own physical health through fear of being or becoming ill.

OBSESSIVE-COMPULSIVE DISORDER: Recurring, distressing thoughts or urges that lead to a felt need to 'put things right' by performing rituals or mental neutralizing.

BODY DYSMORPHIC DISORDER: Marked concern about one's physical appearance accompanied by excessive worry about it.

POST-TRAUMATIC STRESS DISORDER: Intense fear that something threatening or injurious, which has happened, is going to happen again.

* Health anxiety is sometimes divided into Illness anxiety disorder and Somatic symptom disorder.

If you have been formally diagnosed with an anxiety disorder, it is wise to sit lightly with the label. As a complex creature, you are always more than a set of symptoms. Let the label defer to you rather than the other way around. The usefulness of any diagnosis is determined by how you relate to it:

• If the label is an honest signpost for doing some necessary work on yourself, then it's helpful.

• If it is something that becomes an excuse for not doing that work, it's not helpful.

• If it is something that raises your curiosity about who you are and what life is about, then it's helpful.

• If it is something you use to define yourself, then you're missing the point.

The word 'diagnosis' comes from the Greek *dia-gnosi*, which means 'to know through'. The original term hints at how the identification of a problem, rather than being reducible to a set of objective facts, is known through the way we look at it. So how might we look at our anxiety without prejudice or presupposition, in order to see it for what it really is? Here we can turn to mindfulness, a clear and spacious 'way of seeing', and an invaluable ally in our quest to live well.

How might we look at our anxiety
without prejudice or presupposition,
in order to see it for what it really is?

EXPRESSIONS OF ANXIETY

❖

The prevalence of anxiety is reflected in the many idioms and turns of phrase that slip off the tongue. We are steeped in the language of anxiety and fond of using its imagery. Each of us knows anxious states so well we often talk about them without realizing it.

To be a 'BUNDLE OF NERVES', have your 'heart in your mouth' or your 'blood running cold' all imply anxiety. Similarly, being at your 'wit's end', acting 'like a cat on a hot tin roof' and, indeed, 'having kittens' also hint at its disordered feel. What all these phrases have in common is that they convey a sense of embodiment. When I say 'I broke into a cold sweat' or 'I felt the ground opened up underneath me', I am describing visceral experiences. I know others will understand me because they know them too. We all have flesh and blood in common.

Through self-enquiry, I have learned a lot about my own pattern of anxiety. Whatever the trigger might be, the 'felt sense' is always the same – waves of heat and tension build within my body, which paradoxically feels stiff and frozen. My chest seems to tremble as my heart thuds and my breathing quickens. I become flighty and fidgety, prone to speeding up actions, skipping over my words, and restlessly pursuing certainty or completion. At such times, my whole being feels narrow. I tend to cut myself off from others. My mind fixates

---

If way to the better there be,

it exacts a full look at the worst.

THOMAS HARDY
1840–1928, NOVELIST AND POET[5]

---

on what is bothering me and screens out a wider view of things. I am capable only of fleeting contact with the world.

When anxiety is intense, it is like being entombed underground or walled up in an unventilated space. My heart thumps loud in my ears. I feel stifled and crave oxygen. I am assailed by notions of being unable to cope. An image that often leaps to mind at these times is of my body, tightly bound, being forced, head first, into a furnace. It is strikingly similar to religious and mythological depictions of hell. To be trapped, suffocating, and destined only for more of the same are common characteristics of hell: the definitive state of 'no way out'. But here my analogy breaks down because what happens to my anxiety next is always the same – it passes. Just because I think something is hell doesn't mean that it is.

The Friendly Force of Mindfulness

A mindful approach to anxiety begins with a willingness to turn towards it – to explore it, to feel it, and to receive it without resistance. You can do this gently, by degrees. You don't have to plunge headlong into the middle of the furnace.

It is more useful (and satisfying) to become acquainted with anxiety step by step – in the same way you might get to know a prospective friend or partner. Through a process of gradual familiarity, you learn more about your relationship with it and, by extension, more about yourself.

The obvious place for a 'first date' with anxiety is your body. Anxiety is an embodied state and mindfulness is an embodied practice – what a perfect match! When you next experience anxiety, deliberately pause and, as best you can, pay attention to how your body feels. Notice the sensations that are present and where they are in the body. Allow yourself to feel them. It will be helpful to make a note afterwards of the 'symptoms' you observe. This allows you to start detecting patterns. Note-making will also help you develop a degree of objectivity towards your experience.

When exploring embodied anxiety in this way, there is one crucial thing to remember: have no agenda. Get to know your anxiety for the sake of getting to know it. That is all. It is rather like trainspotting, if you consider what trainspotters do *and* what they don't do. Trainspotters carefully observe and make notes about the details of passing trains. They do not try to stop, divert, derail or in any way interfere with trains. Their participation is precise in its nature – just watching, with curiosity, what is happening before their eyes. Do the same with your anxiety – watch it and feel it without interference or resistance. What do you discover?

MEDITATION

SAYING HELLO TO ANXIETY

❋

When you feel anxious and it is possible to go somewhere quiet where you won't be disturbed, take ten minutes to do this exercise. Dedicate two or three minutes for each instruction.

• Sit in an upright, relaxed posture and gently close your eyes. Take one or two deep breaths. Then allow the breath to return to its own rhythm. Take a few moments to become aware of your whole body.

• Where in the body do you notice anxiety most intensely? If there are several areas of the body, choose the most intense sensation. Give it your full attention. Explore this sensation closely. Let go of any thoughts about it. Feel the feeling directly.

• Where does this feeling start and stop? Does it feel hot or cold, or both? Is it on the surface of the body or inside? Does it move or pulse? Does it stay still? Does it have edges? Is it constant or changing? Is it one sensation or a range of sensations? Explore it with curiosity. Find out everything you can about it by feeling it directly.

• Now imagine this feeling was an object. What would it look like? Allow any image or images to form in your mind in their own way. What shapes, shades or colours come to mind? What textures? Observe this object with interest.

• Allow yourself to have this feeling. Make room for it. You don't have to like it. Notice that your body is big enough to hold this feeling. Notice that your mind is big enough to make an object out of it. When you finish this meditation, make some notes about your experience of it.

SUCH STUFF AS DREAMS

Fertile ground for investigating our anxiety is our dream life. The unconscious bears great relevance to our conscious experience. Listening to what is happening in our depths fosters awareness. As in waking life, anxiety in dreams can take many forms, from missing a bus or sitting an exam to being stalked by a monster. The more you explore, the more patterns you will find.

RISK OF PHYSICAL DANGER is a common way for anxiety to express itself in a dream. Here, the danger is aimed at the 'you' in the dream (whoever or whatever you may be). This may be a direct threat, such as feeling yourself falling or something hurtful being aimed at you. Or it may be indirect, perhaps a distant danger or a natural disaster, such as a fire or an earthquake, taking place. Many people report waking up during such dreams, which is indicative of wanting to escape from their anxious feelings.

Dreams of being pursued by something shady or malevolent also signal anxiety. Upon waking, the inclination can also be to 'run away' from thinking about such dreams. Might it be possible instead to reflect upon them? After all, whatever seems evil to the 'you' in the dream can do you no harm in broad daylight. Spending time with dreams can be a creative pastime, which adds depth and colour to waking life. Dreams seek no end meaning, just like poetry.

KEEPING A DREAM DIARY

✳

Time is of the essence when recording dreams. Their mercurial nature is such that your recall of them breaks down in seconds and minutes. Here are some suggestions for good diary-keeping:

• Keep a notebook and pen within reach of your bed. Record the dream the moment you wake up.

• First, quickly run through the whole dream in your mind. Then write down every detail. Even if your recollection is vague, still write it down.

• Details might include colours, moods, atmospheres, characters, symbols, shapes, actions and interactions with other people or things.

• Record every fragment, no matter how insignificant it seems. Find an extra word or two to describe particular feelings or vivid scenes in the dream (exciting, scary, heavenly, etc).

• Stick to a written description (content, imagery and mood). Do not interpret, embellish or judge.

• Give the dream a title – something that captures its main theme(s) – and write the date beside it.

Kissing Frogs

A dream pursuer may represent a natural desire for unconscious material to become conscious. This indicates a healthy shift taking place in the mind. The anxiety felt in the dream is, therefore, predicated on the running away 'you' do in the dream and, by extension, the avoidance of it you apply when awake. If you stop running from the dream, you allow your unconscious mind to move on. Even better, if you can stop running *in* the dream, you may find the pursuer also stops – or changes beyond all recognition.

Working with dreams is greatly assisted by having no agenda. Resist the temptation to seek a definitive interpretation. Let a dream speak its own language, allow it to reveal itself.

Lightening the Load

Over several years I had recurring dreams about losing bags. The prevailing atmosphere was always consternation turning to panic. I mentioned them to a therapist friend, who suggested I keep a 'dream diary'. Soon I noticed a common aspect to each bag dream – my relentless search to locate the missing luggage, which always resulted in finding only a part of it, and an accompanying sense of dissatisfaction.

In one dream I was on a beach strewn with thousands of bags! I hunted for mine, becoming frantic and exhausted. Eventually I found what I thought was mine, but it was somehow 'not quite right'. I woke up with a feeling of frustration and heaviness. When I reported this dream to my friend, she said: 'You might feel a bit lighter if you gave up trying to carry all your baggage around with you!' It was such a simple observation yet something 'clicked' for me. The frequency of the dreams declined, although I'm still working on 'letting go'.

CHAPTER TWO

CATCHING
YOUR BREATH

*Anxiety is necessary for the preservation of
life. Too little anxiety in dicey circumstances is
as disordered as too much anxiety when danger is
non-existent. Finding the willingness to live with
uncomfortable feelings is the smart path to take. We
can get real about anxiety by understanding how the
mind works and developing the gently powerful skills
of mindfulness. We can learn to take care of ourselves
in ways that keep us connected to life's joys. It is
possible to cultivate an inner versatility that is
both liberating and heart-warming.*

HOW TO GET ON A ROLL

◆

In our search for security, pleasure and meaning in life, we encounter obstacles. This may provoke unwanted feelings of nervousness and apprehension. But if we struggle with these feelings, we only add to our stress. We also run the risk of setting up a cycle of anxiety — and getting stuck there.

ANXIETY MANIFESTS IN MANY DIFFERENT WAYS. Often it comes and goes and you think nothing more of it. But if anxiety keeps recurring, either with excessive intensity or disproportionately to the situation, this indicates that something has gone awry in your relationship to yourself or the world. This is a cue for some inner work. A good place to start is getting acquainted with how anxiety cycles work.

All anxiety cycles are composed of interacting mental, emotional, behavioural and physiological factors, all propelling each other. A cycle starts up, is self-perpetuating for a period of time, and then stops, only to restart later. Every person's anxiety cycle is unique, but they all share the same basic components:

• You detect a potential threat. This could be anything: a situation, object or entity in the outside world; a thought in the mind; a feeling in the body.

• You interpret the threat as explicitly hostile, intolerable or disastrous.

• You selectively focus on the threat. You remain on the look-out for it. You seek to detect it as quickly as you can.

• You experience a 'felt sense' of being in danger.

• Your body undergoes rapid physiological change in response to nervous arousal.

• You seek to control your experience. This can take many forms: changing, checking or manipulating things around you; attempting to change, check or manipulate thoughts and feelings; seeking assurance or certainty from yourself or others.

• You seek to avoid or escape the threat altogether. You remove yourself from it and calculate how to avoid it in the future.

Such is the speed and complexity of your psycho-physical functioning that you won't distinguish between these different components at the time. When a cycle activates itself, everything seems to happen at once. Of the points listed above, you may only be conscious of aspects of the last two, which concern how you act and react. Control and avoidance are understandable but they are also counterproductive because they 'close the circle' and set up the conditions for the cycle to recur.

Risking Change

Some anxiety cycles are best worked on with professional help. Others are resolvable through your own efforts. You have to make your own choices. Whatever route you take, determination and skilful action are required. As a therapist, I have

---

When a great ship is in harbour and moored,

it is safe, there can be no doubt. But that is not what

great ships are built for.

CLARISSA PINKOLA ESTÉS
POET AND PSYCHOANALYST[6]

---

worked with many people struggling with anxiety. I am always struck by how it imprints differently on each person's life. For one person, it might be a specific fear of a particular object or place. Others might wrestle with doubts about their own mind, or a lingering state of dread about being alive. What everyone shares is a willingness to turn towards their discomfort. This is a prerequisite for moving beyond it.

In helping people overcome their fears, I have found myself doing many peculiar things. Once, I circumnavigated a roundabout fifty times in a car with a woman seeking to overcome her fear of driving around it. I have walked in parks and on hills, stood on bridges and ridden buses with people who were convinced they would collapse, go crazy or die in these places. At other times, I have invited clients to 'put me in harm's way' – for example, having one hold a knife to my throat for an hour at a time so that he might conquer his fear of harming others. Whatever the 'experiment', my clients always found their fears to be unfounded. They had to take risks to discover that for themselves.

Stress Relief

A confrontational approach to troublesome anxiety is often not necessary and is certainly not the norm. However, some emphasis on behavioural change is always helpful. Remember that anxiety is about perceived threat. Threat induces tensions in the body and mind. Without shrewd intervention on our own behalf, we will accumulate and carry around these tensions, which precipitate stress and prompt more anxiety. It is common sense to take the pressure off however we can.

Since the time of Hippocrates (460–375 BCE), the 'father of modern medicine', people have understood the benefits of treating anxiety with fresh air, healthy diet and a balance of rest and exercise. What you put into your body affects your mood, energy and mobility. Even just a few minutes a day of aerobic exercise changes how the body regulates stress hormones. Contact with nature and time spent on hobbies are vital to your welfare. Sustaining healthy change requires wise attention and effort. The mental qualities of wise attention and effort lay the foundations for a mindful life, which is carved from a judicious consideration of cause and effect.

Action Points

Left unattended, anxiety cycles tarnish quality of life. Here are some guidelines for restoring mental, emotional and physical well-being by bringing awareness to day-to-day experiences and enacting new intentions:

• TAKE ONE STEP It is easy to feel overwhelmed thinking about the future. Breaking down goals into small steps cuts through indecision and procrastination. Make a list of things you want to achieve in the immediate future. Beside each item, write the next step you need to take in order to complete the task. Aim to complete small steps regularly. Each time you do, write down the next step. Small, consistent actions drive you forwards and make the future look 'doable'.

• JETTISON EXCESS If you are struggling to keep up with everything demanded of you, try activity monitoring. Keep a written record, hour by hour, of everything you do. At the end of each week, review your record. What are you doing excessively? When and how are you 'busying' yourself unnecessarily? What can you change? Plan small adjustments, using the minutes and hours as your time frame.

• LEARN TO RELAX A natural inhibitor of anxiety, relaxation is a skill to cultivate. Find a self-help programme or devise your own. It should include some regulation of activity (changing routines, taking breaks, etc) and exercises that involve directing attention to particular parts of the body and tightening/releasing of muscles. NB Do not confuse relaxation exercises with formal mindfulness training. They have different aims.

• SAVOUR THE GOOD Give special attention to positive events and pleasant experiences that occur. Otherwise it is easy to overlook or dismiss the pleasures and joys of life. No matter how small they might seem, soak them up and reflect upon them. Dedicating a notebook to all the 'good things' of life will help to reinforce your efforts. Documenting the causes for good things happening is an accessible way to explore your interconnectedness with the world and cultivate gratitude.

• PRACTISE GENEROSITY This is a natural antidote to the mental contractedness that stems from fear and consternation. Generosity takes many forms, from the giving of time and attention to the sharing of material resources. Energetically, it is a 'giving outwards'. It loosens you up. It opens your heart. It connects you with things beyond yourself. It makes life nicer for everyone, you included.

• CONFRONT DOUBT Dithering and back-peddling are the fuel and fallout of many anxious states. If you are not putting your full energy into things because of uncertainty, lay down a friendly challenge to yourself. Choose something you are wavering over. Commit yourself to act. Act! Just do it. See what happens. Now bring the same attitude to something else you are hesitating about.

• ASSERT YOURSELF Be honest with yourself and with others. You have a right to be heard. So have they. If you have difficulty making requests, practise using clear language such as 'I would like you to…' and 'Please would you…?' Experiment with making clear, economical statements and note how that feels. Drop words like 'perhaps' and 'maybe' where possible. In disagreements, start sentences with 'I think…' and 'I feel…' rather than 'You think…' and 'You are…'.

THOUGHTS ABOUT THINKING

◆

There is an old Zen story about a man on a horse, which is galloping at breakneck speed down a road. Another person, standing by the side of the road, shouts to the horse-rider: 'Where are you going?' 'I don't know!' comes the breathless reply, 'Ask the horse!'

LIKE MANY GOOD STORIES, this one is about more than at first appears. The horse refers to the human mind. It is an apt metaphor. Like horses, minds are sensitive and curious creatures. They are spirited, frisky and temperamental. They are able to settle, be patient even, but at any point they are liable to rear up and run off.

One way minds hightail into the beyond is through the medium of thought. If left unchecked, thoughts chain from one to another into strings of ideas and random associations, and the effects on mood, emotions and actions can be profound. Thoughts carry a degree of emotional charge. Similarly, your thoughts are reflected in how you feel. For example, thinking scary thoughts leads to feeling anxious and feeling anxious gives rise to scary thoughts.

The interplay of thoughts and feelings unfolds so fast we are rarely aware of it, and one innocuous notion can lead to a profusion of hopes, fears, dislikes and desires. Your inner life can cover vast expanses in moments, leaving you reeling, wondering what's going on. Your horse has bolted.

Walls Cannot Contain Me

I once worked for a social outreach project in rural Asia. The centre, where I also lived, provided healthcare and education for local people. It was surrounded on all sides by rice fields and was crudely demarcated by a waist-high wire fence. The view across the fields was enchanting – flat, green lushness as far as the eye could see. In my free time, I loved to hop over the fence and walk around the patchwork of paddies, revelling in the space and tranquillity. My work could be tough, but I rejoiced in the connection with the people and with the landscape. There was a prevailing sense of contentment in my life. My mind was often quiet.

Unfortunately, the centre's location made it a target for armed bandits, who twice raided it during the night, coming across the fields to rob residents of money and goods. This impelled the project managers to commission the building of a nine-foot brick wall around the centre, with iron gates and a lookout tower. My world changed. Now I was living in what felt more like a prison camp – walled in all day, rifle-toting guards on patrol, and no visible sign of the beautiful nature

---

Whatever one pursues with their thinking and
pondering, that becomes the inclination of their mind.

THE BUDDHA
FIFTH CENTURY BCE[7]

just metres away. Averse to my new surroundings, I grew agitated. I knew the fortifications were necessary and I knew I was safe inside the centre, but my mind never stilled in the way it once did.

Later, I realized that my changed mental state had less to do with brick walls and bandit raids than with the way I was thinking. My mind had taken to brooding over the loss of that idyllic view and the free access to the paddies. It didn't accept my new circumstances and jabbered relentlessly about 'the way things used to be'. When I went for daytime walks by way of the front gate, I would huff to myself about how 'it's just not the same any more'. My liveliness was sapped by all this mental bustle. If that wasn't enough, I started worrying about my loss of contentment and inventing new hazards that might befall me. Despite never having been safer from bandits, my mind seemed bent on tangling itself up in negative futures.

This experience proved a good lesson in how my mind can kidnap itself and gallop off into misadventures of its own making. Brick walls are an effective way of repelling external threats but they make no difference to an inner world besieged by non-acceptance and lost in its own projections. Now I try not to hold unrealizable expectations about the changing environments of my life. I keep more of an eye on what is happening 'inside'. To maintain a balanced appreciation of life requires me being alert to my unruly mind and learning how to ride it well.

EXERCISE

CONTAINING CATASTROPHE

❋

Worrying minds tend to think 'What if..?' thoughts. It is a futile attempt to secure certainty about the future. When you notice your mind is in a 'What if..?' cycle, you can uncover its hidden assumptions by changing the question to 'So what if..?' Pose this question to your mind and listen to how it replies. No matter what your mind comes back with, stick to the question 'So what if..?'

Example: Having the worry 'What if I don't get paid on time?' > *'So what if I don't get paid on time?'* > 'I won't be able to afford the rent…' > *'So what if I won't be able to afford the rent?'* > 'I'll become homeless…' > *'So what if I become homeless?'* > 'I'll lose my job and end up begging…' > *'So what if I lose my job and end up begging?'* > 'I'll get sick from the cold and collapse alone in the street…' > *'So what if I get sick from the cold and collapse alone in the street?'*…

Keep challenging the mind until it runs out of assumptions or gives up. Expect it to create multiple worst-case scenarios and ever more exaggerated, catastrophic visions of the future. This is what minds do.

If you arrive at a baseline assumption that seems both realistic and probable, ask yourself three questions: How many times have I worried about this in the past and been wrong? Is it the end of the world? What can I do about it?

Non-Proliferation Strategies

Thinking is a primitive form of action which, like any kind of action, has consequences. Occasional thoughts can repeat to become habitual. Habitual thoughts shape mental traits and, in so doing, subtly shape character. This happens quietly, gradually, moment by moment, day by day, via the innumerable judgements of the ever-active, thinking mind. Becoming aware of this process exposes the sheer saturation of thought in one's life. It reveals the emotional substrate to our thinking, which normally goes unnoticed. It also shows us how the mushroom clouds of proliferating thought affect how we feel and how we act.

Formal mindfulness practices, which encompass a range of meditative techniques, share a common thrust of taming the restless human mind in kindly, patient ways so that we might act in ways that make us feel good. Fundamental to this endeavour is working skilfully with thought and how it relates to our wider experience. We begin to see how emotions build up, expressing themselves via ideas and impacting on our physicality and behaviour. Mindfulness practice is about letting go of potent tendencies to indulge thoughts and to create a fixed identity out of them. Bringing awareness to self-generating cycles of neurotic thinking robs them of their momentum.

Formal mindfulness practices ... share a common thrust of taming the restless human mind

Mindfulness leads to a disenchantment with all the arbitrary content that rolls through the mind. Paradoxically, this grants a greater flexibility and creativity for one's life.

True Reflections

One escape route from webs of proliferating thought is through conscious reflection on thoughts themselves. When you are experiencing anxiety, deliberately stop what you are doing and take a look at the thought-stream running through your mind. If necessary, write down the thoughts you spot. Find out everything you can about what is bothering you. Then give your full attention to the following questions:

• What is the main concern here? Does it have any foundation? What am I afraid might happen?

• How does this concern affect my life? What other aspects of my life does it connect with?

• How useful is it to think in this way? What are the benefits of thinking in this way? What are the drawbacks?

• What would it be like if these thoughts were not here? What would I give my attention to instead?

• What can I do about this concern? Would my actions be driven by urges to avoid uncomfortable feelings or would they be appropriate and practical ways of addressing the issue? Now resolve to follow through on an appropriate and practical course of action. Or, if you conclude no action is needed, determine to give your full attention to your next activity.

MEDITATION

WATCHING THE MIND

❋

- Sit in an upright, relaxed posture. Let your back be relatively straight, without straining. Let your eyes gently close. Take time to become aware of sensations throughout your body.

- Gently direct your attention to the sensations of breathing. Feel the rhythm of the breath, the flow of air into and out of the body. Notice the whole cycle of breathing, including any pause before each in-breath. Allow the breath to be as it is.

- Now let go of the focus on the breath and bring full awareness to what is happening in the mind. Become an observer of your mind. Watch whatever arises – images, ideas, words, memories, fantasies, mental impressions. Observe without getting involved.

- Thoughts and images will arise. When they do, don't resist them or engage with them. Simply watch whatever occurs without interference or judgement. Unhook from all topics and content of thought by tuning in to the *flow* of thinking.

- Relax. Allow awareness to be broad. Notice the spaces between thoughts – the tail end of one thought and the gap before the next thought arises.

- Pay attention to what abides in your experience between thoughts. If no thoughts or images appear, notice their absence. Let the mind rest in this open expanse – the space from which all mental phenomena arise and dissolve.

- Practise sitting quietly in this way, allowing everything to pass through. If you become distracted, bring your attention back to the breath, notice one or two breaths, and then resume observation of the mind.

MIND GAMES

Investigating anxiety reveals intriguing truths about the workings of the human mind. Threat responses are hardwired. Learned habits and tendencies can seem equally fixed. We like to think we are in charge of our inner world when, in fact, the mind is running on autopilot much of the time.

WHEN WAS THE LAST TIME YOU NOTICED how you opened a door? Or sat in a chair? Or any other actions you undertake time and again? All those countless micro-movements of muscles, tendons and ligaments, informed by intention and will, seem to happen all by themselves, right? You've got more important things to focus on than opening doors, right? And just what were you focusing on when that door was opening? Can't remember? 'Somewhere else', were you? That's normal. It's how minds work. From one moment to the next, as life unfolds with blistering novelty and ambiguity, it's tricky to know where the mind is at.

Minds are so incredible they are impossible to explain. Or locate, for that matter. Are these words you are reading inside your mind or outside your mind? If they are inside your mind, how come they're out here, on this page front of you? If they are outside of your mind, how do you know they exist? Rather than pose head-crunching riddles, let's try broad brushstrokes instead.

Your mind is a rapid and spontaneous flow of experience with no boundaries – bodily sensations, thoughts, feelings, imaginings, urges and fantasies all flowing into each other. Your mind is a life-preserving machine – it is constantly scanning and focusing on things in order to create momentary coherence out of fragmented sensory impressions, which allows 'you' to make sense of things and to survive. Your mind is your world – it runs manifold simulations of past and future while creating a virtual reality of everything outside of your skin. In short, your mind is a self-reflexive entity that is profoundly sensitive and oddly unknowable. It defies rational explanation.

Going Through the Motions

Much of the time, minds take care of things without ado. Faced with attention-demanding tasks, they are conscientious in their execution of physical and mental action. During such times, there will be an immediacy and freshness to your life. On other occasions, when nothing particular appears to be happening – what we might call 'downtime' – minds remain on the go. They reflect, introspect, replay events, assimilate new learning, craft plans, conduct moral reviews, even rewrite and update a kind of rolling autobiography. Minds never stop. They are the ever-present yet inconspicuous repository of all experience. They provide consistency and clarity through an ongoing processing of events that orients

'you', moment by moment. It is your mind that is making sense of these words right now.

Problems arise with how minds get locked into inflexible ways of behaving. One example, pertinent to this book, is how minds reach into the future, seeking to know what is going to happen next, only to induce feelings of disconnection from the here and now. Another powerful tendency of minds is to wander. They do so constantly, without warning, and without awareness they are wandering. This wouldn't be so bad if minds always drifted into happy thoughts or creative reflection, but they wander much more frequently to neutral or negative content (due to some primitive hardwiring in the brain). This kind of inattention triggers fruitless daydreaming and, more harmfully, impulses to brood and worry.

One sunny afternoon, sitting in a lecture theatre during an interval in an enjoyable presentation, an uneasy feeling descended upon me from out of the blue. When I turned my gaze inward, I caught a glimpse of a mental pattern that was pervasive and long-standing: when there is nothing wrong, nothing to fear and no problems arising, my mind scans around, looking for a problem to latch on to. I then experience a nervous feeling, which can easily coax me into a deeper discontentment. This was an insight into the staggering power of my mind to slide from a contented state to one of angst in a finger snap. It showed me how anxiety steals its way into my peaceful world unless I am wise to it.

EXERCISE

FULL STOP?

✳

Try this exercise for a straightforward glimpse into how your mind works. Read the following instruction carefully:

• When you get to the end of this sentence, focus your eyes on the full stop after the word 'up', stay right there, don't do anything else, and watch what shows up.

• Now you are reading this sentence. Did you catch the moment when your eyes moved from the full stop? Was that movement intentional or did it seem to happen by itself?

• Now cast your mind back to when you *were* focusing on the full stop. What happened? What did you experience?

Would you like to try the exercise again? Please do. It will be different this time.

Life in the Fast Lane

In their continual efforts to make sense of everything, minds over-extend themselves. They get so focused on what might happen 'up ahead' that they lose track of what is happening now. The mind splits from the body and leapfrogs into a future time and space. This is a hallmark of 'doing mode', which is a kind of goal-focused state habitually favoured by human minds.[8] Doing mode is necessary for getting things done, but it engenders a loss of 'presence' and the vividness and wonder that come with being present.

Another downside to the mind in doing mode is its overblown attempts to problem-solve things that can't be solved. Take, for example, a state of anxiety. Often anxiety arises when there is no tangible threat and no action needed, but the mind still makes a problem out of it. It focuses on the gap between how we feel (anxious) and how we want to feel (not anxious). It searches for explanations for the anxiety and tries to eliminate it. This requires the mind to fixate on the very feeling it is seeking to get rid of. At these times, the mind does not seem to know that feelings cannot be erased, only felt. The mind's attempt to control the uncontrollable leads to the persistence of the very thing it is wrestling with: anxiety.

This roving mind, forever trying to figure things out, is prone to getting stuck in loops. Being perpetually on the go, engrossed in outcomes and roaming the gap between 'here' and 'there', is tiring. It feels like competing in a never-ending greyhound race – propelling oneself around and around the same old tracks, chasing undernourishing cuddly toys. Surely there is more to life than non-stop doing? Surely the mind can apply itself in more inspiring ways? There is and it can.

Nothing fixes a thing so intensely in memory

as the wish to forget it.

MICHEL DE MONTAIGNE
1533–92, ESSAYIST

LIGHTNESS OF BEING

◆

To be takes practice. If I forget to stop, wait, listen and let go, I become less of a human being and more of a human doing (a humbler species). To claim my full birthright requires me to experience life in its immediacy, rawness and breadth. Finding ways to do this can seem heretical in a world bent on ambition and achievement.

WORKING AS A THERAPIST is a wonderful opportunity to sit with people and to work with whatever shows up, whether it be uncomfortable, ambiguous or awesome. On one level, I inhabit the same world as my clients. They bring me their problems and struggles, but they also bring me mine, for aren't we all hindered and mortal creatures, hustling through life, prone to anxiety, dissatisfaction and confusion? On another level, our worlds are different – each client has their experience, I have mine; they are working on a personal matter, I am doing my job. So we sit in our togetherness and our separateness and chew over what is going on.

We explore the client's issues from different angles and what these mean. Often we experiment with new ways of relating to problems. Yet 'solutions' often emerge organically, in ways neither of us could imagine and often when we least expect them to. Positive change seems to come more through *being fully with* what shows up in one's life rather than trying to dispose of problems.

The wisdom of the changes my clients make is testament to their willingness to inhabit themselves more fully. Their work in therapy furnishes healthy inner change. One client, who was habitually anxious, transformed her life by getting up early, walking to work (instead of driving), stopping en route to drink tea in her favourite park and to take a photograph to remind herself of the spaciousness she felt there. A self-employed man, highly stressed yet hooked on overworking, forced himself to take proper holidays by stapling together the relevant pages of his work diary in advance. Another client, prone to harsh self-attacking, learned to relate to herself with more compassion when she pondered on the effortless kindness she had for her child at the dinner table.

Small Change, World of Difference

The changes these people made in their lives have two things in common. First, they arose spontaneously out of their inner work. Second, they are a means to stopping and gifting space to oneself. Just taking a photo, stapling pages or feeding a baby can change one's world if it arises from – and, in turn, nourishes – a heartfelt wish to be on better terms with oneself. It has nothing to do with gain or glory; it's more about wanting to dwell in the immediacy of one's life. This is a hallmark of 'being mode',[9] an inconspicuous but ordinary state of mind characterized by accepting and allowing things to be as they are, without pressure to change them.

Being mode is indefinable but, suffice to say, you are probably in this mode more than you realize and not as much as would be good for you! Being is about presence. It is the aliveness you feel through purposefully paying attention to what is happening *now*. It is the sense of childlike wonder when you see something for the first time. It is the poise you find when you are grounded in your body and alert through your senses. It is foremost about a particular way of paying attention. Attention, by its nature, is virtuous because attending to something, anything, is to value it. Nothing is possible without first giving it attention.

Most of the time we are in doing mode – mentally focusing on the gap between where we are and where we want to be. Striking a harmony between doing and being is a healthier balance. If life is a journey composed of expectations, plans and goals (doing), might we also attune ourselves to this step – the one we are taking right now – on our journey? Giving attention to how we take each step, rather than fixing on our destination, is to access our capacity to be. When we do this, the journey feels richer. And we see a lot more along the way.

No Time Like the Present

To enter being mode, first you need to stop, outwardly and inwardly. Then, drop into the body to sense fully what is happening. You can do this any time. How about now? When you finish reading this paragraph, stop what you're doing (reading and everything else). As you let go of all doings, let your shoulders, jaw and belly relax. Allow awareness to open to your embodied experience. Listen inwardly to what is happening in body, heart and mind. Let thoughts glide by. Allow yourself to *be fully in* the totality of experience and consciously *aware of* it too. This is a position of being both a participant and an observer. Hang on to nothing. Just be.

Life abounds with natural interludes, like the space between one paragraph and the next. They are the punctuation points of life. When we deliberately pause, we grant ourselves an opportunity to relax amid the stream of events before making an intention about where to take life next.

Public Space

My favourite symbol for 'just being' is a park bench. Park benches are simple, accessible structures, open to everyone and owned by no one. They are intimately connected to the natural world and free to use anytime. They are resting places on journeys from here to there. They allow us to stop, inhabit space and orient ourselves. For me, park benches serve as a gracious reminder of the importance of pausing, connecting and opening up to my experience. What symbolizes 'just being' for you?

WHAT'S THE STORY?

At times writing this book, I have noticed how my attention strays from the sentence I'm working on and catapults itself into a future time when the book is complete. It invariably lands on one of two well-established scenarios, whips out the relevant script and plays it like a movie.

ONE MOVIE GOES LIKE THIS: 'I've finished the book. It reads great. I feel great. Life is wonderful. The end.' The other movie synopsis is: 'I've finished the book. It's a mess. Everyone hates it. I'm a failure. The end.' Sometimes both scenarios play out together, like two stories edited into one nonsensical blockbuster.

Regardless of which movie is on, there comes a point when I realize my attention has drifted. With that realization comes an organic return to my here and now experience. The film dissolves and I am back writing this book-in-progress. The feelings I experience depend upon which movie has just been showing: buoyed up if it was the 'great book' one; uptight and uneasy if it was the 'failure' one; confused if it was both. Whatever the feelings, they soon fade to nothing.

This process neatly encapsulates some core themes of this book. Our minds have a tendency to stray into imaginary futures. They tell tales that are crude fictions. They often do this without warning. This tendency is not helpful, especially

> The mind never stops oozing and spurting
>
> the sap and juice of fantasy, and then congealing this
>
> play into paranoid monuments of eternal truth.
>
> JAMES HILLMAN
> 1926–2011, PSYCHOLOGIST[10]

if the imaginary future is a disagreeable one. But all is not lost! Human minds also have the ability to notice themselves, their content and their straying behaviour. In so doing, they are able to regain their focus and retrieve a perspective on the present that is not cloaked in fantasy. This is mindfulness in action: the mind's innate capacity to recollect the present moment and to attend to the task in hand.

The 'Should' Life

Mindfulness has benefits beyond just being focused enough to complete actions. One of its many other assets is the capability to not take the babble of the mind at face value. Minds automatically concoct stories and construct views of self and world based upon the conditions of the moment. To be alert to this requires the practised art of handling these mental narratives with a pinch of salt. Some of the stories we tell ourselves, about ourselves, ride long-established, well-worn grooves in the psyche. They tend to be negative and judgemental, and are therefore liable to make us feel ill at ease.

Here we tap into a rich seam, deep within every human, of anxiety. Consider the myriad ways we assess, judge, label and measure ourselves as being 'OK' or 'not OK'. The sharp words we sling at ourselves when we don't meet with our own approval. What about all the times we secretly compare ourselves to others, desperately try to 'fit in', or push ourselves to perform to certain standards in order to feel acceptable? Everyone craves attention, success and respect because we care about how we appear to the world. We fear rejection for the same reason. We worry what other people think of us. We worry if other people don't think of us. The confirmation we seek is many-sided but, ultimately, is all about 'me'. The fear of being deemed 'not good enough' and the striving to be 'good enough' are two sides of the coin that is the self.

Our search for self-validation has troubling side effects. We develop unconscious assumptions and expectations about how we (and others) should and shouldn't be. We berate ourselves if we don't meet our own standards (and do the same to others when they don't measure up). Judgement cramps the mind, making life into a chilly and inhospitable affair. Our tendency then is to become vigilant to threats, the source of which is actually within – one part of the self is scolding another part of the self. At such times, one of the many clunky versions of the 'not good enough' story is being played out within the psyche. Anxiety is being, literally, self-created.

Taking in the View

For my mind to conjure a story about writing this book that reduces me, wholesale, to the status of 'failure' says more about how my mind works than it does about 'me' (I hope). How can the multitudinous experiences, roles, actions and identities over decades of existence — all of which go into making up this entity called 'me' — be reducible to a single, negative evaluation? Alas, assigning generalized labels is something my mind does.

The good news is that arresting this tendency is also at my fingertips. I don't have to identify with the facile constructions of my clumsy mind. Its restless and idle nature will only lead me astray. Mindfulness provides an antidote to this because, when I become aware of the mental story, it ceases to gain any footing in my mind. The 'I'm a failure' belief is revealed by awareness to be a gross distortion and so loses its emotional energy. The story finds its proper place in the order of things — just one more passing plotline in the rolling soap opera of the self.

Judgement cramps the mind, making life into a chilly, inhospitable affair

Developing a mindful approach to the aversive mind enables me to better negotiate its many misrepresentations of 'me'. When I do this, I get a strong hint of not just the mental versatility that mindfulness contributes to my life, but also its warm and compassionate embrace.

MEDITATION

MINDFULNESS OF DISCOMFORT

✳

• Find a quiet place to sit down, back relatively straight and body relaxed. Allow your eyes to close and bring your attention to the sensations of breathing in your belly. Let the breath breathe itself. Let your experience be your experience.

• Now deliberately open up to what is uncomfortable. Silently name the feelings (e.g. 'anxiety', 'unhappiness', 'frustration'). Is there more than one feeling? Are there clusters or cocktails of different feelings? Notice and feel how they express themselves in the body. Go right into them.

• Allow yourself to be present to all of these feelings and sensations. Sit with them. Breathe with them. Give them all the space they want. Let go of mental stories about these feelings. Let them be as they are.

• Do you notice urges to get rid of these feelings or to end this meditation? Are you tensing up or resisting in any way? Notice in the body where you feel urges to 'get rid of'. Bring your attention directly here. Can you see how the urge to get rid of, or move away from, is distinct from the feeling itself?

• As you become aware of the interplay between the feeling and the reaction to it, let the attention be partially with the breath as well. Breathe with the feelings. Breathe with the urgency to move away. Make room for the discomfort. Open up to it all.

• Let thoughts flow and pass. Be with your experience, patiently and kindly, moment to moment. As long as the discomfort is present, let it be. If the discomfort subsides by itself, let it go.

TENDER IS THE NIGHT

Anxiety is characterized by losing one's head. Mindfulness is characterized by not losing one's head. In that sense, they are very different states. But the gap between them is subtle and easy to miss. The distinction boils down to the stance we take towards what is happening within our minds and bodies.

THIS WAS BROUGHT HOME TO ME by two very different encounters with anxiety on consecutive nights. The gloomy hush of the bedroom is an ideal place to catch the turmoil of the mind when it has nothing else to occupy it. How easy it is to get stranded in a mire of aversion when the mind works itself into a frenzy. What a subtle shift it is to step out of the mire altogether.

Monday. 11pm. I am in bed, relaxed, cosy and sliding towards sleep. An innocuous conversation with a work colleague from earlier in the day pops into my mind, like something sparking randomly inside my head. My body twitches and contracts. There is an aching wish to not think about work. Too late – I'm focusing on the thought, replaying it in my mind. As I do, seemingly against my will, memories of work scenes, people and tasks sprout and mushroom. Thoughts about tomorrow niggle and scratch. The cinema of my mind plays a madcap biopic of the rest of my life. All the things I have to do! But all I want to do is sleep.

My body tenses in resistance to this mental kerfuffle. My heart seems to flutter and bubble under the contours of my skin. There is a rush of adrenaline and I am launched, shocked and appalled, into full wakefulness. Tomorrow sweeps in like a suffocating fog, filling the blackness of the room. All the things I have to do! Plans, projects, problems vie for attention in this crowding head-space. My mind tosses and pitches in a sea of impending futures, all buffeting each other like angry waves. Muscles quiver in my body, restless limbs wrestle with the duvet. My eyes bulge, stomach churns, throat grips. All I want to do is sleep. Give me sweet oblivion, *please.*

A Hostile Takeover

Anxiety, fully fledged, announces itself like a wild cat pouncing out of the darkness, pinning me down and clawing at my windpipe. Nervous system stuck on arousal now. My heart is like a fist in my chest. Threat alerts fire in my brain. Thoughts flare and explode in multiple scenarios of tomorrow, next week, next year, inventing ever more undesirable outcomes, concluding nothing beyond the necessity to keep thinking.

My mind is on the run now, careening out of control, no recollection of where this all started… Something about a work colleague, was it? No time for that – there are worries to be worried and problems to be pondered from every angle, over and over again. Somewhere, it seems, in the airless crush of my skull, I am boxing myself senseless.

Hours pass. I lie staring at the ceiling, restless and aggrieved. A mental image arises of a bony, disembodied hand rapping harshly on a glass door in the basement of my mind. I wince at its jarring message to give up on sleep forever: 'Stop chasing rainbows, you loser. You are not drifting away. There is the whole disturbing occasion of the rest of your life to deal with.' I concede to be exiled, first to the arid plains of doubt and despair, later to the choking volcanoes of rage. The blustery winds of anxiety never abate. The spectre of tomorrow edges forever closer as clocks tick in all directions, their hands hauling me, wide-eyed and exhausted, through the dust of the night.

A Rescue Mission

Tuesday. 11.30pm. I lie in bed, staring at the ceiling, in wilful opposition at still being awake. 'I am *so* tired. Not a wink of sleep last night. Here we go again! Worked too much today. Why didn't I take a break? Why do I never learn? I've over-done it. Another night of ruin. And what about all the things I have to do?' A pang in my heart. A jolt in my shoulders. The mental torment seems relentless: 'I'll be wrung out tomorrow. What if I never sleep again? I won't be able to face anything. Why has this happened to me? What if I never sort this out? I'll be doomed...' These thoughts spin and whirl again. In its careless attempts to flee from them, my mind blunders into them all the more.

All of life's conflicts are between letting go
or holding on, opening into the present or clinging
to the past, expansion or contraction.

CHERI HUBER
ZEN TEACHER[11]

I catch what's happening. The agonizing. The catastrophizing. The mind slipping out of reach. But I *see* it. I wake up in a different way – to what is happening. An intention arises, one forged through years of practice, to remember my body. I feel this tingling frame of tissue and bone from the inside out. The touch of the bed covers, the sensations of pressure from the head to the toes. I remember to feel my breath – the ebb and flow of the air in my belly, calming in its nature. Within the wrapping of my skin, a world of sensations begins to open up. An intricate life of feelings declares itself. My poor, demented mind may be captivated in its hall of mirrors, but there is a whole lot more going on if I care to take a look.

A Tranquil Release

I have some perspective now. I have descended from the attic room of thought into the animal of my body. This creature opens doors for me like a generous host, offering smooth passage into its humble abode. I am no longer fleeing my experience, but arriving into it, over and over again. And behold

— a cathedral of sensations and pulsations, temperature and pressure, and blessed space. There is room for everything. There is room to breathe.

Not everything is pleasant. The body expresses its tensions. The breath feels tethered, coarse, trembling high in my ribcage. Like a defiant dog, the mind refuses to lie down. But there is a newfound openness to its unruly ways. I watch with quiet eyes the flow of impressions that is life, without the need to control or shape them. I find a willingness to explore the edges of hostile thoughts and the crampings of flesh. This feels like cutting through all the churning to a deeper stillness underneath. I harness the mind with a simple question – 'How does this feel?' – and I let myself feel it, whatever it is.

Time lengthens, things quieten. The mind begins to settle. I rest the attention on the breath and use it as a touchstone from which to fully experience whatever is showing up. There is a stream of sensations. There is the flow of out-breath and in-breath. Things know how to take care of themselves if I let them. I renounce all demands and expectations, even to go to sleep. In a state of indisputable peace I dwell lightly with an intention to be present. In time I drop even this intention to slip into unconsciousness. Hours pass in oblivion before my alarm clock jangles to life and throws me, fresh and bright, into a new day.

Things know how to take care of themselves if I let them

CHAPTER THREE

FINDING REFUGE

*The best way of taking care of the future
is to take care of the present. We can do this through
mindfulness practice — the cultivation of a range of
mental qualities that includes attention, interest,
equanimity, tranquillity and effort. Mindfulness offers
a way of experiencing life without the descriptive overlay
of the chattering mind. It confers vitality and insight
through sensitizing us to the interconnectedness of body,
mind and world. We learn to become a reliable witness
to what is going on. Putting the past in its rightful
place and engaging skilfully with life now better
equips us for whatever is coming next.*

HOME IS WHERE THE HEART IS

In times of danger, we need a safe place to turn to. In times of stress, we need solid ground to rest on. A mindful approach to life neither denies nor contests the changing conditions we encounter, but it advocates a refuge resilient enough to cope with them all.

I ONCE WROTE AN UNDERGRADUATE THESIS on Vietnam War movies. This required me to immerse myself in the imagery of that war and its story on celluloid. But in all of my research, a single photograph made a greater emotional impact upon me than all the movies put together. Nick Ut's *The Terror of War* is a snapshot of Vietnamese children fleeing a napalm attack on their village in 1972. Centre of frame is a naked, screaming girl, badly burned by napalm, running down a road. She is traumatized. The girl, Kim Phuc, survived her ordeal and went on to become an ambassador for peace. The picture, as photojournalist Horst Faas put it, 'doesn't rest'.[12] It haunted me from the day I first saw it.

Twenty years later, I better understood why. A colleague mentioned another famous photograph, this one taken in 2001, of terrified New York citizens fleeing across the Brooklyn Bridge as the towers of the World Trade Centre collapse in the background. She told me a story about the trauma specialist, Dr Bessel van der Kolk, who showed this photo to a group of psychotherapists. 'Where are the people in the picture running to?' he asked. After several puzzled moments and quizzical stares from the students, van der Kolk answered his own question: 'They're going home.'

Any 'running from' something, out of fear, is also a 'running to' somewhere: shelter or sanctuary. Instinctively, when facing grave uncertainty, we run to where we feel secure and towards those whom we love. We call this destination 'home'.

Shared Humanity

When my colleague told me the story about van der Kolk, I recalled the picture of Kim Phuc and, for the first time, fully grasped its haunting power. It was not possible for Kim Phuc to go home. Hers had been razed to the ground. You can see it in the background of Ut's photo, reduced to a billowing mass of black smoke, quietly transmitting the little girl's deeper tragedy of having nowhere safe to run to.

Viewed in this way, the effect of the photo is to leave the viewer stranded in the middle of a dangerous road with a terrorized and wounded child. It is an arresting image that speaks not just of the obscenity of war but of human vulnerability and existential insecurity. Facing mortal threats, humans need to run. Life distils down to survival. Seeing the suffering of others, we can open our hearts. Life broadens with compassion. Implicit, here, are connections between primal human drives of witnessing, feeling and acting – all of which are fundamental to mindfulness practice.

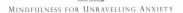

Everybody needs a home. It is a part of human nature and pertinent to any authentic enquiry in how to live peacefully, with ourselves and with others. From a mindfulness-based perspective, such an enquiry needs to include not just what is happening around us but also the conflicts and struggles we wage within ourselves.

The Meaning of Refuge

Existence continually obliges a response from us. This is true not just for what is happening around us, but for what is happening within us. Thoughts, feelings and sensations arise and we react, sometimes adaptively, sometimes not. The human propensity for anxiety highlights our susceptibility to grave *internal* dangers, in the form of troublesome mental habits and impulses, which lead to suffering. How best to respond to these? Where can we find safety? We need a place to go that is robust and versatile enough to withstand the ever-changing problems we face or create. We need a refuge.

We are always taking refuge in something, often without realizing it. Many of the ways in which we direct our lives are unconscious attempts to find security. We take refuge in people and places, beliefs and ideals, work and hobbies, alcohol and drugs, money and status, pleasure and distraction – not to mention all the inventive ways we have found to avoid pain and discomfort (for a while). But how reliable are these pop-up shelters we erect along the paths of our life?

We find refuge whenever our
hearts open with tenderness and love.

TARA BRACH
PSYCHOLOGIST AND MEDITATION TEACHER[13]

It takes honesty and courage to look at what we put our faith in and to consider how leaky the roof might be.

To be true, a refuge must be a safe haven from *all* imaginable threat. It should also offer more than respite from instability and turmoil by serving as an ongoing assessment of one's priorities in life. It should, therefore, be wedded to one's core values and to the aspiration to live with optimum ease. Nor is a true refuge totally separate from its occupant. It is more a means to 'coming home' to oneself – to know oneself wholly and to realize one's true nature.

A Secure Base

Mindfulness practice offers the possibility of such a refuge. In the most general sense, to be mindful is to take refuge in awareness. Awareness is the ever-present, boundless container of your life. It is the clear and open space through which you know all phenomena. Mindfulness is about intentionally becoming more and more aware, but in such a way that is, paradoxically, a non-achievement. You don't need to acquire awareness. By giving up on notions of acquisition, you let awareness shine through. Like the air around you, awareness is all-encompassing, readily available and easy to miss.

To dwell in awareness is to orientate yourself in a certain way. There is a conscious shift away from the mind's tendency to concretize time and to conceptualize the ensemble of psychophysical material that comprises self and world. The emphasis is on immediate experience. There is no need to ignore the past or deny the future – by grounding yourself in the here and now, you simply let go of mental stories the mind tells about time. This gives rise to a particular way of seeing: receptive, connective and non-interfering in nature. You are free to approach life as you might look upon a work of art – situating yourself in it and allowing it to reveal itself.

Such a way of seeing is a non-judgemental gazing at life without a sense of ownership. Dwelling in the always-new experience of each moment is to move beyond the confines of ego and to open up to the interacting and interdependent

---

We never look at just one thing; we are
always looking at the relation between things and
ourselves. Our vision is continually active, continually
moving, continually holding things in a circle around
itself, constituting what is present to us as we are.

JOHN BERGER (1926-2017)
ART CRITIC, NOVELIST AND PAINTER[14]

---

nature of existence. You become sensitive to the flow of things without making them personal. This forges a deep, steady connection to what is happening within and around you. As the psychotherapist Joseph Zinker puts it, through awareness you learn 'to listen ... without wanting, to touch without desiring, to love without squeezing, to gaze without becoming overly pedantic'.[15] Kindness and compassion flow naturally from the refuge of mindfulness. Coming home is heart-opening.

THE TERRITORY OF MINDFULNESS

In life it is easy to get disorientated, sometimes to lose our way entirely. This is true when treading the path of mindfulness. If we confuse the map for the territory, we risk reducing the art of mindfulness practice to some glib definition or simplistic technique. Good signposts and reliable guides help to negotiate these pitfalls on the path.

GETTING A CLEAR HANDLE on the concept of mindfulness is tricky. The word is used variously to describe a mental quality, a psychological process and certain contemplative practices. None of these are easily conveyed in words. For this reason, mindfulness is prone to getting shrivelled into limp definitions of the 'be here now' variety. Yes, its practice does involve inhabiting (i.e. being) what is not absent (i.e. here) in the presenting moment (i.e. now). But it is about much more besides.

Tantalizing clues hide in plain sight. Look up the word 'mindful' in an English dictionary and you will find its definition extends beyond 'being conscious' to include 'taking care' and being 'of good memory'. It was all three meanings, not just the first one, that inspired nineteenth-century translators of ancient Buddhist texts to coin the term 'mindfulness'.

If you want a three-word definition for mindfulness, 'holding in mind' is more fit for purpose than 'be here now'. 'Present moment recollection' illuminates the important link between mindfulness and memory. To be mindful is to *recollect* what you are engaged in now. Recollection literally means 'bringing together' and 'finding again'. Mindfulness exerts such an integrating influence. It stitches together your immediate experience out of the jumble of sense impressions that are in constant flow. Mindfulness takes care of life by bringing its breadth and complexity into sharp definition.

Mindfulness also has a monitoring and stabilizing effect on the mind. It is a witnessing of phenomena *in relation to* phenomena. Through its non-superficial observation, mindfulness fuses a bright awareness of the present moment with a knowing that this moment does not exist discretely – it is continually drawing on the past and giving way to the future. To be mindful, then, is to occupy a unique position amid the stream of existence, neither getting lost in the stream nor being apart from it. A mindful stance has one foot in time and one foot in the timeless.

EXERCISE

HOW TO HAVE A HAPPY ENDING

✳

A simple and versatile way to cultivate mindfulness is to pay attention to the end of an action. You can do this with any activity, no
matter how small or routine, such as setting down a cup, switching
off a machine or closing a door. Deliberately pay attention to the
dying moments of the action. Be in your body and awake through
your senses as you notice the cup coming to rest, the machine going
quiet or the click of the door. Witness what is happening – a mini-
ending, both complete and gone for good. Registering this allows
you to move more fully into the next moment.

Fresh Fields

The subtlety of mindfulness is such that the architect of its
practices – Siddhattha Gotama (fifth century BCE), known as
'the Buddha' – employed diverse similes to illustrate its character. He likened its monitoring and recollective aspects to
the careful gatekeeper of a town; its knowledge-gathering
properties to a surgeon's probe; its detached observation to
the climbing of an elevated platform; its balancing effect on
the mind to carrying a bowl full to the brim of oil on one's
head; and its stabilizing nature to a post strong enough to harness wild animals.[16] An inspection of the Buddha's teachings
highlights the importance he attributed to mindfulness,
an ordinary mental quality with extraordinary capabilities.

One bent on their own welfare should
practise mindfulness and guard the mind.

THE BUDDHA
FIFTH CENTURY BCE[17]

The Buddha mapped out four fields for the cultivation of mindfulness – body, feelings, states of mind and mental phenomena – which provide the 'how' and the 'what' for all forms of practice, ancient and modern. Their shared invitation is to open your eyes, face reality and work out how best to deal with it. Their encouragement is to renounce futile agendas to escape the unpleasantries of life, and instead find the strength to be as sensitive as you are. Skilful practice leads to insight – a knowing that undercuts all limiting inner narratives and that 'sees' the nature of phenomena directly.

The language of 'seeing' permeates mindfulness teachings. In terms of meditation practice, to dwell in the mystery of being alive – the emptiness and fullness of the perpetual now – is to look in wonder at this strange and ephemeral world as if for the first time. By dropping all preconceptions we can witness what is really going on. When we look in this way we discover that ordinary experience is as astonishing as it is ungraspable. It is the way a child might look upon an object it has never encountered before – with openness and curiosity, but without the baggage of interpretation and association.

A pivotal moment in Siddhattha Gotama's life story is an experience in childhood when he was quietly observing events. One day, sitting beneath a rose-apple tree and watching his father ploughing a field, he spontaneously entered a refined state of consciousness. Recalling this event years later provided the catalyst for his becoming a 'Buddha' – an honorific title meaning 'one who is awake'. The distinctive quality of Siddhattha's experience under the rose-apple tree – a particular way of paying attention – was the key to his awakening.

State of Nature

Mindfulness practice works by side effect. When I think of 'mindful moments', what come to mind are not all the meditation sessions and intensive retreats I've done over the years. They are the times when I'm walking in a wood or a park and the presence of nature seems to open up, lucid and vibrant, around me. Or when I spy a fox or a cat scrutinizing me from a hedgerow and everything seems to stop while we exchange curious glances, utterly alive to the other. Or times sitting by a river, seeking nothing, when boundaries dissolve and there is just rippling water, solid earth, transparent sky. These moments of small wonder, unplanned and fleeting, are deeply unifying yet unattached to anything. They do not belong to me, which is what makes them so special.

Meet the Locals

Mindfulness practice leads gradually to a transformation of attitude, new understandings and changes in behaviour. If we look closely at what constitutes this practice, we find a range of mental qualities – not just mindfulness – which are allied to each other. First, the commitment to practice requires some degree of trust – not only in the practice but also in one's own abilities. Then, three specific qualities provide the necessary energy for one's practice: the unshrinking application of effort, the willingness to investigate, and the joy of interest. Three other qualities maintain the stability of one's practice: steadiness of attention, the tranquillity that comes from stilling the body and mind, and the unshakeable balance of equanimity.

Learning to recognize these qualities is an art in itself. Tranquillity is not passivity. Equanimity is not indifference. Such discernment opens the mind up to wisdom.

It is mindfulness that monitors and helps to develop these allied qualities to such powerful effect. When mindfulness practitioners talk about feeling extraordinarily balanced, focused and calm, they are actually referring to a harmony of mental qualities, where mindfulness itself is the balancing factor. Such uplifting states are a by-product of good practice. They naturally incline the heart towards kindness, compassion and joy. The effects of practice radiate outwards, informing how one moves and acts in the world at large.

MEDITATION

ABIDING IN AWARENESS

✳

- Sit in a relaxed, upright posture and gently close your eyes. Establish an overall sense of your body. Open up to the space around it. Open up to the space within it. Notice the full range of physical sensations. Notice their qualities of pressure and temperature. Let go of preferences. Be with the breadth of your experience.

- Tune in to the flow of breathing. Don't try to change or control it. Observe the coming and going of each breath in its own time. Simply observe and feel it. Let your body open to the flow of breathing and the subtle changes associated with this flow.

- Bring a watchful awareness to the passage of thoughts and mental impressions. Do not chase, grab, resist or struggle with any of them. Step back and observe the show. Let the parades of mind-objects come and go. When you get caught up in something, notice the moment you unhook. This moment of 'stepping back' *is* the practice.

- Now open up to whatever feelings, moods and emotions are present. Be *with* what you are feeling. This is different to being *in* the feeling. Let go of stories and judgements about feelings. Stay with their overall flavour, tone and movement. Give them room. Breathe with them. Feel how they resonate in the body.

- Keep grounding awareness of body, mind and heart in the present moment. Receive each moment with impartial, open interest. Let go of notions of past, present and future. Dwell fully in the immediacy of what is happening now. Let everything arise, remain and vanish in the quiet expanse of awareness.

MINDFULNESS OF THE BREATHLESS

◆

Mindfulness meets anxiety in an intimate encounter on two fronts.
It seeks to know the direct experience of anxiety and all the inner
reactions to it. Mindfulness opens up the gap between the raw phys-
icality of anxiety and the mental patterning, conditioned through
past events, it precipitates. Attuning to anxiety in this way means a
new relationship with it becomes possible.

O N THE FIRST MORNING OF A WEEK'S HOLIDAY, I acciden-
tally stood on a rusty nail. It went squarely into the
ball of my foot and hurt like hell. The pain churned nauseously
with agonizing thoughts about the possibilities of infection.
With help, I cleaned and bandaged my foot and got a tetanus
jab. Then I got to work on my mental state. I acknowledged
the event had happened and could not be undone; that it
could have been a lot worse; that I'd be able to walk properly
again soon. By the evening, I had dealt with my worries and
come to terms with my predicament. Or so I thought.

The next day, fresh waves of anguish tore through me. The
mental stories about being incapacitated swelled into an
ocean of resistance. Negative thoughts washed across the
grievous swamp of my mind. I drowned in my own deluge.
Only when I probed deeper and got down to the underlying
root of my problem – the mental grasping at work – did I
restore some inner balance.

Up Close & Impersonal

Look deeply into the process of mind and what becomes apparent are habitual patterns of liking and disliking, wanting and not wanting. These are primordial impulses, collectively known as 'grasping'. The human mind grasps in two ways: desiring and rejecting. Desiring is the urge to seek more of and to cling to. Rejecting is the reverse desire to get rid of or to get away from.

When we mindfully investigate this mental push and pull, we begin to see its obstructive and imprisoning effects. The grasping mind solidifies and exaggerates the gap between the way things are and the way we want them to be. It vacillates between pursuing the desirable and fleeing the undesirable. The consequences are far-reaching – compulsiveness to obtain, grief of loss, fear of loss, frustration and disappointment when we don't get what we want, to name but a few.

Mindfulness practice provides a release from this unconscious tyranny. By tuning in to the deepest currents of the mind, stopping short of identification with their content, we get right up close to what is happening without getting stuck to it. Through the power of equanimity, we come to see how our normally blind reactions give rise to grasping – how pleasant feelings lead to desire and unpleasant feelings to aversion. We discover how grasping fuels mental proliferation and painful emotional fallout. We find a different place to stand, safe from the smash and grab of the mind.

One does not become enlightened by imagining
figures of light, but by making the darkness conscious.

CARL JUNG
1875–1961, PSYCHOTHERAPIST[18]

A dynamic shift takes place through this newfound receptivity to our inner life. Awareness is freeing. The vicious cycle
of grasping, exposed for what it is, loosens and relents.
The mind still flows. Emotions retain their creative function.
What is different is how we respond to events inside and out
– more flexible, more skilful, more open to change.

Anxiety Laid Bare

The penetrating gaze of mindfulness offers new vistas on anxiety. It cuts through mental prattle and blind emotional
reactivity to the bare experience itself. It sees the unpredictable and fluid nature of feelings, how they express themselves
as turbulences in the body and how they colour the mind.
Mindfulness grants us access to the building blocks of reality.
We dive underneath our preconceptions of 'anxiety' to examine its living parts: perception, meaning, hedonic tone,
impulse, sensation, reaction. Becoming a curious observer
with no axe to grind enables us to let go of tendencies to build
an identity out of transient states. Like any befriending exercise, mindfulness practice is about getting better acquainted.

A common mistake made by mindfulness practitioners with anxiety issues is to expect to achieve states of calm through meditation. This is a form of grasping – a seeking to indulge in pleasant states and to avoid the unpleasant. A wiser orientation would be to appreciate (and investigate) calm states when they do arise and to treat anxious ones with great kindness and respect. The radical encouragement of the practice is to sit with the most disagreeable of states for as long as they last. Sooner or later, they exhaust themselves of energy.

Five Hindrances

An essential reference for all mindfulness meditators is the traditional scheme known as the 'five hindrances': sensual desire, ill will, dullness/drowsiness, restlessness and doubt. These are normal features of psycho-physical experience, which obstruct the brightness and agility of the mind. When we get caught in these states, our minds tend to clutter up and dis-engage from the present moment. These states, however, are not enemies. They are energies to be worked with, even welcomed because they are bringing to light deep mental habits. Much of the skill of meditation involves engaging with these states in such a way that they cease to be a problem.

Anxiety is its own peculiar blend of all five hindrances but its primary constituents are restlessness and doubt. With restlessness, we need to be patient. Try to flick it away and we just keep firing it up. Better to use the energy of restlessness to investigate its fluctuating nature. Doubt, a state of being pre-occupied with uncertainty, if worked with skilfully, is a valuable ally for examining the changing nature of experience. In this way, hindrances are instructive company. Mindfulness practice involves working with – never against – all states of mind. Its liberating prescription is to accept, no matter what.

A DEAFENING SILENCE

The art of mindfulness meditation – opening up, being curious, staying friendly – is easier said than done. During a silent retreat, I discovered how simple it is to stray from the boundaries of good practice and to get lost in tangles of my own making.

THREE WEEKS INTO A MONTH-LONG RETREAT, I was well acclimatized to the elegant economy of dawn-to-dusk meditation sessions. The conditions of a residential retreat have a special quality to them. There is nowhere to go, nothing to do. Freed from work demands and other pressures, my mind was relaxed and alert. Life was as quiet as falling snow.

Well, except for my tinnitus, that is. As a long-time sufferer, I am practised in the art of screening out the sound by focusing my attention elsewhere. But in the deep stillness of the retreat, acutely sensitive to all sensory contact, I was unable to distract myself. The tinnitus became the dominant presence in my world. It would mutate into outlandish music and build into deafening throbs. Discordant symphonies and medieval war chants would emerge out of ungodly white noise to create strung-out, tuneless dirges. Hour upon hour this cacophony pounded between my ears. Sometimes I could not get to sleep. The more I fixated on it, the louder it grew.

Theory & Practice

My meditation teacher pointed out that this was my mind playing tricks – fabricating music out of mere sense-impressions. Rather than resist what was happening, he encouraged me to explore the raw, unadulterated sound and my subtle mental reactions to it. Intellectually, I knew it was good

Meditation Retreats

Meditation retreats are a traditional form of intensive mindfulness practice. They are held at retreat centres, usually located in rural areas, and last from several days to several months. They are conducted in silence. A retreat is an opportunity to devote yourself to meditation practice in a way not possible in normal life. A typical daily schedule involves continual sitting and walking meditation interspersed with some sleep and food. There is the added encouragement to practise mindfulness of all routine activities, such as eating, bathing and doing chores.

advice. In mindfulness meditation, the focus is on the act of hearing, not the sound heard, in order to see how the mind overlays the bare sensory experience with ideas and judgements. I had lost sight of the first principles of good practice.

I rallied myself for a new focus of meditation – to observe closely the arising and dissolving streaks of sound and witness how my mind fashioned tunes out of emptiness. The theory was good, but I had not reckoned on the colossal power of mental grasping and the strength of my unconscious agenda to get rid of the 'music'. Consequently, within hours, I had reduced myself to an anxious and angry wreck. Ready to rip my own ears off in revulsion to the sonic bombardment, I spent an entire day in a state of acute distress, cursing my decision to ever go on retreat. Worries multiplied about living the rest of my life to a soundtrack of whistling kettles and white noise. By the next day, I had become convinced that I was going deaf from the barrage.

Author of My Own Suffering

At this time, some new people joined the retreat. Given the small size of the centre, I was aware of their presence – new faces, smells of urban life on their clothes, the speedy ways they walked. In the meditation hall, I could not help noticing how they shuffled on chairs and cushions. I began sensing how the person sitting behind me would fidget on his cushion. Another man at the back of the hall seemed to breathe noisily.

I grew frustrated with these unsettling newcomers. They seemed so disturbing. My meditation depreciated to a gluey state of self-absorbed brooding: 'Who *are* these people? Why won't they shut up? They're ruining my practice. Why is it that every time I go on retreat, there's always someone who breathes like a drain? And why is it that the person sitting behind me has to be the most restless one in the whole room – rummaging around like a hamster in its sawdust...'

Off lurched my mind, drunk on self-pity, to tumble into a sinkhole of ill will: 'These people have no respect. Don't they realize that some of us have been here for ages? It was fine before this lot came along. They are ruining the whole atmosphere. They don't care. How selfish is that! And here's me with the added challenge of my tinnitus...'

When I finally clocked this mental diatribe for what it was – a torrent of gross exaggerations and nonsensical implications – it stopped dead in its tracks (to be replaced by the inner burn of embarrassment and shame). I had seen through the mental mirage to what was really going on – my tinnitus was no louder than it had ever been. Nor was I going deaf. If I could hear people breathing and cushions rustling, then my ears were working fine! The only thing disturbing my retreat was my own aversive mind.

In mindfulness meditation, the focus is on the act of hearing, not the sound heard

WHAT'S IT ALL ABOUT?

The path of mindfulness is not just about meditation. It is about everything that comprises ordinary life. The way we speak and act, where and how we work, what we do and with whom — all lie within the sphere of 'practice'. There are many ways to develop an open heart and pliable mind. Just remembering to try is half the effort.

THE PRACTICAL MEANS TO CULTIVATING MINDFULNESS fall into two major categories: formal and informal. Formal practice refers to specific forms of meditation. Regardless of the precise technique, all formal practices concern the development of a range of wholesome mental qualities, which quietly support one's everyday life. Meditation promotes emotional resilience and psychological flexibility in a similar way to how exercising in a gym promotes muscle strength and physical endurance – the benefits come indirectly over time. Progress goes unnoticed, at least for a while.

Informal practice refers to being deliberately aware of whatever activity you are engaged in. Anything from eating a grape to emptying a bin can be a means to cultivating mindfulness. *How* you do something is what matters. It is all about intention and attention. Formal and informal practices entwine to support each other – meditation is potent fuel for the clear knowing of what you are doing as you are doing it; being more present in everyday activities contributes depth

Daily Practice

Regular meditation practice is the only sure-fire route to experiencing the benefits of mindfulness. Outer conditions are important – a quiet place where you won't be disturbed, something comfortable to sit on, and audio instructions (or a timer to signal the end of the meditation). One practice period per day, minimally of 15 and optimally of 45 minutes, is a good yardstick. Preferable is two daily practice periods – one in the morning (to set the mind up for the day) and one in the evening (to help the mind digest the day). Once a solid meditation routine is in place, remembering to punctuate the day with moments of deliberate stopping (to 'be') becomes easier.

and clarity to meditation. A mindful life, then, is about forging a dynamic balance between being and doing. It is not some exotic lifestyle choice. It is about getting real with existence.

It's Not What You Think

Popular notions about the mystical or transcendent nature of meditation are misunderstandings that derive from a confusion between how something looks from the outside and the actual experience of it. Formal practice is a far cry from stereotypical media images of beautiful people sitting cross-legged

on beaches, basking in serenity. In its bona fide form, meditation is about embracing the warts-and-all of life and letting go of urges to have it any different. It has overtones of what the poet John Keats (1795–1821) called 'negative capability', a term he used to describe the human capacity for 'being in uncertainties, mysteries, doubts, without any irritable reaching after fact and reason'.[19]

Meditation is also a purification of the heart. It lifts the lid on the mind's suppressive tendencies and allows emotional turbulences to express and expend their energy. Good practice hurts – sometimes! By providing the tools required for releasing the accumulated tensions that come from being human, meditation is an on-the-job learning in how to move beyond the constricting habits of a lifetime. To assist one's efforts, courses, retreats, sitting groups and experienced tuition are invaluable resources.

Informal practice, in contrast, does not involve diving deeply into our psychology. It is about being aware of intentions. It is about remembering that the only action possible is the one we are engaged in right now. It is about active presence. Doing something mindfully is to be wholly absorbed in it, to do it so thoroughly and precisely that we do not notice the passing of time. When we are not lost in mental stories, which by their nature concern past or future, we consciously inhabit the timeless space called the here and now. This is the 'achievement' of practice, as humble as it is profound.

Something so simple is, of course, easy to miss. Misapplying mindfulness in an attempt to exert control over the ungraspable now is a common pitfall. Enchantment with imagined ideals of 'being mindful' is another. We cannot perfect mindfulness practice, hence it is called 'practice'. But when we give up on seeking results, we let peace, joy and understanding breeze in.

AN ETHICAL PATH

With mindfulness, confidence grows through practice. Foundational teachings provide a dependable point of reference. Clarity and purpose come through your own reflections along the way. Every step becomes a deliberate and wholesome act.

IF YOU MAKE THE PATH A CENTRE LINE IN YOUR LIFE, it is an education in sensitivity. It leads out of the prison of self-preoccupation to reveal new dimensions to experience. You become more attuned to cause and effect – how the way you act affects your mind, and vice versa. Seeing this leads to making healthy, skilful choices or, at least, to minimizing the painful impact of selfish, ignorant ones. The influence of mindfulness practice extends from the solitude of formal meditation to quietly effecting change in the world.

Here, the mental quality of mindfulness moves beyond its capacity for cultivating active presence to assume an ethical

---

Be careful of your words, for someone
will agree with them. Be careful of your conduct,
for someone will imitate it.

LIEH-TZU
FOURTH CENTURY BCE, TAOIST MASTER[20]

---

function. By recollecting the effect of actions (or mental states) from the past, it discerns the skilfulness, or otherwise, of actions being taken now. This is akin to having an internalized gatekeeper, cool-headed and wise, who quietly monitors your interactions with the world to enhance your sense of ease and diminish your potential for suffering. Alerted to the disturbing emotional fallout of acting harshly or dishonestly, you are less inclined to pursue this kind of behaviour again. Noticing the calming effect of clear, kind speech means you are more likely to talk that way in the future.

Noble Action

Living in awareness cuts through erroneous divisions the human mind makes between 'me' and 'other', 'us' and 'them'. Anxiety loses its primary foothold when we learn to trust and be trustworthy. We can relax. As we come to know more of our innate connectedness to other beings, we are more considerate in how we treat them. We incline towards activities that align with our values, rather than being swayed by fads and fashions. We reflect on how we make a livelihood and the impact it has on others. We see the sense in rejecting association or involvement with destructive behaviour. When we witness mistreatment, cruelty and injustice, we more readily take a stand against them.

Active engagement with this troublesome world is as much part of 'practice' as appreciating its joys and wonders. Mindful living is not reducible to sitting motionless on a meditation cushion, watching one's breath; it means being dynamically in the world, with eyes wide open.

Such a comprehensive 'taking care' of life is what links mindfulness organically to friendliness – the willingness to move close to, respect and connect with. To be discerning about what we consume, physically and mentally, and thoughtful about what we produce, in both word and deed, is to approach life with open hands and an open heart. Becoming more discriminating in how we take in the world, and cognizant of what we put into it, leads to a more nourishing experience for everyone. Mindfulness takes the form of a rapport with other beings and greater tolerance of the vicissitudes of life. Whatever shows up, we breathe with it, respond intentionally, observe what happens and learn from experience.

Anxiety loses its primary foothold
when we learn to trust and be trustworthy

Good Practice Guidelines

A traditional fivefold scheme to support one's practice is:

- To avoid harming living beings
- To avoid taking what is not freely given
- To avoid causing suffering through sexual behaviour
- To avoid speaking untruths
- To avoid indulging unmindful states through alcohol or drugs

These are not commandments. They are training guidelines. They encourage awareness of one's actions and the effects of these actions. For example, the point concerning intoxicants is not a moral judgement, but a caution about the potential impact on the other four guidelines.

These five guidelines, expressed above as abstentions, also have a flip side. When lived by, they express themselves in their positive aspects, which are, respectively:

- To act with kindness and compassion
- To act generously
- To practise contentment in one's relationships
- To communicate truthfully and recognize falsity
- To act mindfully

Designed to foster a particular attitude to life, such guidelines are the symptoms and products of authentic mindfulness practice.

HISTORY IN THE MAKING

◆

The mindfulness tradition emanates from a timeless past. Old, reliable forms remain intact. New forms, grounded in the old, flow like arteries off a main channel. Contemporary scientific insights into common health problems have ushered in an era of unprecedented interest in mindfulness — and raised new questions.

EVERY PATH STARTS WITH A FOOTPRINT. The first impression on the path of mindfulness was the Buddha's, made twenty-five centuries ago and still fresh today. From his ministry in ancient India, the path has wound its way through continents and cultures, informing and sometimes amalgamating with the indigenous traditions it has met en route. In the West, mindfulness has moved from the contemplative fringes into the mainstream. Innovative models have been developed in the health, education and business sectors. Such was the daring and genius of the Buddha that new models have not deepened the path, rather widened the road. More people than ever have greater access to a living tradition founded on wisdom and compassion — if they know where to look.

The route westwards for mindfulness has been circuitous. The first great advance in this direction took place in the nineteenth century when a mixture of colonialism, scholarship and literature brought the teachings of 'Buddhism' — a term invented by British academics and missionaries — to Europe.

Immigration and a growing interest in Eastern philosophy also played their part. It may be surprising to know that English language books on mindfulness are nothing new. You need only read *An Experiment in Mindfulness*, written in the 1950s by a British naval Rear-Admiral-turned-meditator called Ernest Shattock, for evidence of that.

In the 1960s and 1970s, the creative collision between Eastern mind-body disciplines and enquiring Westerners catapulted mindfulness into the fields of medicine, psychology and spiritual enquiry. Scientific evidence of the benefits of its meditation forms has since sealed its fate as a versatile treatment for a range of health issues. It has been an unlikely journey from the heat and dust of the Indian plains to a clinic and school near you. The archaeologists, scholars, spiritual seekers and medical pioneers responsible for bringing mindfulness within our reach were a courageous and unconventional bunch, with a penchant for posterity – all helpful qualities for anyone wishing to explore, in depth, the ancient path today.

Purchasing Power

As well as finding a natural fit in the field of Western healthcare, mindfulness has become a very marketable product. A lucrative industry has built up around it, trading on both its 'ancient wisdom' credentials and its proven scientific benefits. Mindfulness has been promoted as a 'fix' for everything from work stress and compromised creativity to poor attention and difficulties with making decisions. The business world has led the way with mindfulness programmes aimed at developing 'resilient' workforces (more efficient, less burned-out, better at multitasking). In the military sector, comparable programmes have been devised to 'improve performance' in theatres of war and to train troops and drone pilots in how to better handle the psychological stress that results from killing and maiming people.

What becomes of 'mindfulness' when the principal motivation is to boost financial profit without regard for the systemic causes of work stress or low staff morale? Is it 'mindful' to numb yourself from the inner trauma and outer destruction of your own violence? Hollowed out of meaning, skinned of goodwill, mindfulness deployed for exploitative or aggressive ends is mindfulness in name only. This highlights how easy it is to misapprehend the subtle and multifaceted nature of its practice. As the veteran meditation teacher Christopher Titmuss notes of such co-opting of 'ancient wisdom': 'It only takes some exaggeration of a simple practical tool for the tool eventually to reveal its shadow.'[21]

Anything that is fashionable is susceptible to dilution and corruption. Uprooted from its ethical foundations, mindfulness can, in theory, be utilized for any number of human endeavours, from assassination and burglary to wine-tasting and golf. But when you divorce mindfulness from empathy, compassion and awareness of causality, what results is little

---

If you don't know where you are going,

you will wind up somewhere else.

'YOGI' BERRA
1925–2015, AMERICAN BASEBALL PLAYER

---

more than a highly attentive, egocentric state of mind that is dissociated from the world around. To 'switch off' the heart and disconnect from others in this way is, almost entirely, to miss the point of the practice.

Taking the Mick Out of Mindfulness

The commodification of mindfulness as a 'feel good' therapy prescribed for personal gain now has a name: McMindfulness.[22] Such a package assumes its rightful place in the burgeoning catalogue of problem-focused, goal-orientated therapies designed to soothe overloaded human minds. McMindfulness is a fitting product for an ethically unencumbered marketplace trading on human desire and aversion, but it lacks authenticity for this very reason. It also relegates mindfulness to a bland technique dedicated to attaining 'presence' and so neglects the practice's broader purpose of 'holding in mind', seeing clearly and remembering what is of value. When a practice for cultivating awareness becomes blind to itself – and, by extension, its interdependent nature – the awareness that results is partial and sterile.

Elevating the 'present moment' into some kind of special state, or goal, is an easy trap to fall into. Mindfulness practice may be a worthy antidote to getting unhelpfully lost in the past and future, but it can just as easily lead to getting uselessly stuck in the here and now. Chasing the calmness of 'being present' is usually the cause of this. Conversely, skilful practice is about letting go of any insistence to be present and giving up on acquiring calmness. This is a delicate balance and easy to miss – all the more so if we forget to reflect on what we are doing, practice-wise, and why we are doing it. Wise reflection is essential to mindfulness. When we abandon this and lose our spirit of enquiry, something in our practice dies.

The obstacles are many on the path of mindfulness, but they teach us so much. I have learned the hard way over the years that practice is like walking a tightrope – skill and effort are required and it is possible to lose balance at any moment. I go chasing contentment, only to wind up disappointed. I go chasing 'enlightenment', only to remain ignorant. Guess what happens when I try to be 'a great meditator'! The good news is that when I give up on chasing, balance restores itself and the practice glides. Such moments bring a refreshing humility – I am engaging with something bigger than and beyond 'me'. Practice ceases to be a private affair. Mainlined into the flux of existence, I may even, for a fleeting moment, glimpse my non-separation from this world of beings and the ever-changing mystery and wonder of it all.

CHAPTER FOUR

LIFE BEYOND FEAR

Nothing lasts forever.
Death is the corollary of birth.
Anxiety is the corollary of the self.
This changing world comes to an end,
moment by moment. We forge onwards in an
unquenchable search for happiness and security.
Where is peace to be found? To be mindful is to
realize how much time we spend re-living and
pre-living our lives, rather than just living them.
By inviting us to clarify our inner confusions,
mindfulness practice points to a direct release
from them. This involves facing up to
the way things really are.

INTERROGATING EXISTENCE

The fact of human anxiety is bound up with other facts of human life. We are born naked and helpless into an uncertain world without any notion of how we got here and where we are heading. In time we find our way, hopefully making sense of our life in the process.

BUT WE NEVER ESCAPE THE PRECARIOUS WORLD we inhabit, one that offers few guarantees of the security and prosperity we seek. Nor can we ever know what is going to happen next. As we hurtle through space on this spinning ball of water, dirt and rock we call our home, with time slipping through our hands and the future unknowable, is it any wonder we get anxious? And yet we survive. And thrive.

The uncompromising enquiry of mindfulness inevitably raises a host of questions (and few conclusive answers) about the nature of existence: Who am I? Why was I born? What does my life mean? What happens when I die? Mindfulness meditation, being solely concerned with the immediacy of experience, does not encourage chasing answers to such questions.

Leaving questions unanswered is, of course, different to ignoring them. They are part of the backdrop to the broader project of 'getting real' with life. For example, when meditators discover (as they frequently do) that their experience of being alive is more than their ego and that life is, by extension, oddly uncontrollable and in perpetual flux, they are confronting the same existential curiosities that have enthralled and confounded philosophers for centuries.

Into the Void

Long before the 'medicalization' of anxiety confined its definition to a set of passing moods, the term had a wider meaning. Anxiety was less a problem, more a conundrum. It referred to something at the heart of the human predicament, namely a state of free-floating dis-ease provoked by the maddening futility of being alive. Existential anxiety is a normal human response to the absurdity of this shot-to-nothing life in which we find ourselves. Since the dawn of time, human cultures have grappled with these great matters of meaning, identity, freedom and death.

One famous explorer of life's voids was the Danish philosopher and theologian Søren Kierkegaard (1813–55), often considered to be the first existential philosopher. For Kierkegaard, anxiety was humanity's birthright due to the inescapable possibilities of our being alone and forgotten in the world, threatened by meaninglessness and reduced to nothingness.[23] From this perspective, the raw fabric of anxiety is composed of the eternal possibilities (and probabilities) of our being abandoned, rejected and unloved. Far from getting dispirited about this, Kierkegaard viewed anxiety as necessary for realizing our creativity and finding fulfilment.

Kierkegaard's thought was to have a major influence on the great existential philosophers of the twentieth century, such as Martin Heidegger (1889–1976) and Jean-Paul Sartre (1905–80). Heidegger, for example, examined our bare-bones experience of being 'thrown into' an unpredictable existence that leads to death. Paralysed by uncertainty, said Heidegger, it is easy for us to shy away from living authentically, only to seek security and distraction in worldly things that offer, at best, temporary solace.[24] Anxiety, on the contrary, holds a unique potential for making life meaningful – *if* we can embrace it. Heidegger considered anxiety to be a subtle state, not altogether lacking in peacefulness, and crucial to 'revealing existence' in stark profile. In so doing, he said, anxiety lifts a veil over the innate strangeness of life and ushers in the possibility of real freedom.

Divine Messengers

The existential perspective marks a radical turn for anxiety – it becomes a solution, not a problem. Such a rendering fits well with a mindful approach, which encourages us to never shy away from the dread of uncertainty and insubstantiality,

---

Anxiety is the dizziness of freedom.

SØREN KIERKEGAARD
1813–55, PHILOSOPHER AND THEOLOGIAN[25]

End of the World Show

One of my favourite closing scenes to a movie comes from the science-fiction classic *The Incredible Shrinking Man* (1957). The protagonist of this film with its self-explanatory title is, by now, microscopic in size. He finds himself alone, forgotten and vulnerable under a vast, star-strewn sky. All that awaits him is shrinking to nothing. Death and inconsequence crowd his mind. Then, he has a revelation: how close, how indistinguishable, are the infinitesimal and the infinite! On the brink of annihilation, he sees his true and unlimited nature. Fearless and awakened, he finally understands what it means to be alive. The end.

but to investigate them. The rare value of anxiety is under-scored in the life of the Buddha, whose own existential crisis was instrumental in his discovering the path of mindfulness.

The story goes that, as a young man, his first witnessing of a sick person, an old person and a corpse were the prompts for his quest to find an end to suffering. Such was the potency of these sights that he would later call them 'divine messengers' – if properly acknowledged, he said, they could lead us to a radical awakening. The Buddha's witnessing of a fourth sight – a meditating ascetic – gave him an inkling as to how such an awakening might be achieved.

LOVE AND DEATH

◆

It is not coincidental that the most reliable source of human anxiety is found in the only guarantee that comes from being born: dying. How tempting it is to drift through life, losing oneself in pleasing diversions, shoring up illusions of unchanging predictability, and viewing death as something that always resides at a safe distance.

P UTTING OFF WRITING A WILL is a piece of cake (I've been doing it for years). Statistics show that only a small percentage of people discuss their funeral arrangements before they die. Professionals prepare the corpses of our loved ones for burial and cremation, so sparing us the ordeal. Such are the efforts we make to evade death close up. These are all classic avoidance strategies. Psychologically speaking, they are doomed to failure. No matter how hard we try, we can never shake off the inevitability of our own demise. The uncertainty of its timing merely adds to our unease.

Mindfulness of Death

Contemplating death is a traditional mindfulness practice. It is intimately connected to the contemplation of imperma-nence. The Buddha pointed out how mindfulness of breathing (a common method of practice) can be used for recollecting death, since it is the breath that separates us from death.[26] To be mindful of one's breathing is also to directly acknowledge

In fear of the tomb

All fears find their womb.

BHANTE BODHIDHAMMA
BUDDHIST MONK AND MEDITATION TEACHER[27]

the *ongoing process* of becoming and dying – how breaths come and go, how phenomena arise and cease, how moments are born and pass away.

This is no morbid or nihilistic fascination. On the contrary, mindfulness of death is to embrace an inescapable fact, to prepare usefully for its occurrence and to incite within ourselves the urgency to live well. The more we can welcome death, the more vibrant life will appear. Rather than exist in quiet trepidation, can we embrace the openness and ease that comes from contacting the preciousness of being alive right now? Facing death takes us full circle, back to the first maxim of mindfulness: it may not be possible to choose what happens, but we *can* choose how we relate to it.

Love of Life

As we observe our world coming to an end, moment by moment, what are we left with? What does it *mean* to be present? Mindfulness practice raises its own 'big questions'. If contemplating death can spare us from the fears of a futile existence, might it also awaken us to the value and significance of our

participation in this world of beings? Mindfulness, after all, is about more than just coming to terms with anxiety. It is about undercutting all primitive urges to avoid, reject and disconnect. The quality of mindfulness 'attends to', with care and sensitivity. Its non-interfering, non-coercive gazing upon life implies an active friendliness.

For the Buddha, being mindful was equivalent to acting kindly in the world. Simple reflections, such as how the air we breathe is shared with others, can arouse a sense of intimate connection to those around us. In empathizing with others we find a renewed faith in our own goodness. In this way, mindfulness augments compassion by sensitizing us to our own and others' struggles. Here, the practice of mindfulness entwines with the cultivation of unconditional friendliness, sometimes called 'loving-kindness'. This is the attitude that underpins mindful action. It is a way of contacting and knowing the world through accepting, respecting and moving close to. It is the experience of being 'interconnected' — in the flow of life.

One day, while meditating, for a flitting moment I experienced something of this. Love leaked through the cracks of all my fear and loathing and, right then, I understood, beyond doubt, that it was the *only* response, the *only* approach to life, which casts no shadow and bears no cost. Like a lightning flash, the moment passed and normal service resumed — in-breath, out-breath, in-breath, out-breath. I still forget to think and act in loving ways but deep in my interior there

MEDITATION

DEVELOPING LOVING-KINDNESS

✳

- Adopt a relaxed and alert posture. Close your eyes. Take time to settle. Allow a broad and inclusive awareness of your body. Simply notice, feel and acknowledge your experience. Bring a spirit of acceptance to this noticing. Let go of likes and dislikes.

- Apply a calm and consistent attention to sensations of breathing in the centre of your chest. This is your 'heart centre'. Feel the breath flowing into and out from here. Tune into the tranquil and rhythmic qualities of the breath. The breath sustains and nourishes life. Let it flow.

- Now bring to mind the feeling of being with someone you love. Can you sense the qualities of friendliness, kindness and care within this feeling? Let these qualities merge with the breath as it flows into and out from your heart centre. (If you do not *feel* kindness and friendliness, that's OK – developing their intention is what matters.)

- With the flow of each in-breath into your heart centre, gently empower this offering of loving-kindness towards yourself by adding a simple, good wish, such as 'May I be well' or 'May I be happy'. Imagine it travelling on the breath deep into your heart. Imbue each out-breath with the same good wish for others and imagine it travelling via the breath into the world: 'May others be well' or 'May others be happy.'

- Continue to cultivate this kindly attitude. Allow the breath, the kindly intention and the well-wishing to be one and the same. Let this quality of loving-kindness flow into your heart and radiate outwards, in all directions, first to individuals you know, then people you don't know, and finally to all beings.

remains a glimmer of knowledge, perhaps, that cultivating mindfulness and loving-kindness leads to the cessation of anxiety, animosity and delusion.

VISIONS OF THE TIMELESS

To make any journey requires us to orientate ourselves. Only when we've got our bearings do we look around and take in the view. This is true on the path of mindfulness. First, we invest energy in meditation by taking mental qualities — ones already in our possession — and polishing them with care. Once established in this practice, we use these qualities to help us to see what we hadn't noticed before.

IT IS SAID THAT THE *Path of Purification* — the original mindfulness meditation manual, compiled in Sri Lanka in the fifth century — was inspired by a question posed to the Buddha a thousand years earlier: 'The world is entangled in a knot. Who can untangle the tangle?'[28] Since mindfulness is concerned with subjective experience, 'world' here refers to one's inner world, not just the world at large. The 'tangle' refers to the suffering that arises from our dealings with disagreeable aspects of the world — anxiety, loss, illness and death, to name but a few. The Buddha's response implied that life gets disordered because of the mistaken way we approach it. We 'mis-see' things and, therefore, misunderstand them. What did he mean by this?

An Elegant Chaos

The open invitation of mindfulness is to know things as they come to be. This means, in effect, confronting instability – the fact that existence is neither fixed nor stands still. Its transitory nature means life is inherently creative – things can only come into being because change is the norm. But when we misperceive the unstable as permanent we open ourselves up to all kinds of dissatisfaction. Our attempts to possess, maintain and accumulate things fail to deliver lasting contentment. Our efforts to evade emotional pain expose our persistent vulnerability to them. When we try to exert control over the changing conditions of our lives, we soon discover our limited agency. It all sounds like bad news. But facing up to the unreliability of life and shattering illusions of continuity are exactly what the path of mindfulness exhorts us to do.

It is a radical journey, one there for the taking. In meditation, that initial gear change from 'doing' to 'being' marks just the beginning. From here, the path opens outwards to facilitate a gentle dismantling of treasured notions of self and world as certain, solid and permanent. Subtle truths about interdependence are the revelation, as is the emptiness of the present moment and the freedom that arises from such a 'way of seeing'. The method is the same as ever: sit quietly and watch what shows up. Awareness becomes the blank canvas upon which the flow of all experience imprints itself. There is no need to do anything, simply observe. The way you look

affects what you see, and the way you see affects what you know. Meditation becomes a persistent, conscientious steering of the mind towards realizing its own nature.

The Unmade Experience

Fully fledged mindfulness meditation becomes a vehicle for direct insight into the characteristics of existence. Through its power of 'holding' objects in mind, the quality of mindfulness facilitates an unflinching enquiry into their true make-up. With sustained attention, we pierce through the façades of solidity and substance to spy the empty nature of phenomena, reduced to their bare and fluctuating state. We might glimpse the entire backstage operation of the conjuring show of life – cascading streams of discrete moments arising and vanishing in rapid succession. To witness this ceaseless disintegration, knowing that sense-impressions cannot be controlled or possessed, is to let go. In letting go, it is said, what arises is an invincible peace.

This is what the Buddha called *Nibbana* – the extinguishing of all suffering and a state of clear, easy contentment. He described it as 'unmade' because it is neither contrived nor dependent on other conditions. It is a quality of radiant attunement that anyone can know – perhaps one we *already* know, except that we overlook it through 'mis-seeing'. Those who consciously know this state describe a newfound appreciation for life in all its forms and a happiness of a different order.

There are those who discover they can
leave behind confused reactions and become as
patient as the earth; unmoved by anger, unshaken as a
pillar, unperturbed as a clear pool of water.

THE BUDDHA
FIFTH CENTURY BCE[29]

Here, it would seem, lies our holy grail – liberation from anxiety and dis-ease in all its manifestations. Whether we think this possible or not, might the example of others inspire us to step up our practice? Remember that the delicate fusion of means and ends on the path of mindfulness dictates that all waymarks are equal. There are no hierarchies. No prior attainments are necessary. *Nibbana* is hard to see only because it is so close, not far away. Our humblest efforts to be mindful lead us into the vicinity of this unshakeable freedom.

Bee Here Now

I remember one afternoon, deep into a retreat, abiding sumptuously content in a world as vibrant and dissolving as a shooting star. I was mindfully walking, at a snail's pace, on some decking outdoors. Rain had cleared and a late summer sun shone its rainbow colours through congregations of silky clouds. Nature everywhere glistened in crystal beauty. Dwelling in a pristine state of undistracted wakefulness, I perceived no limits,

only shifting states of space and form where nothing was missing and nothing was out of place. Awareness held the universe as soft as a tuft of cotton wool.

Under these conditions of unobstructed receptivity, everything appeared lucid and precise – the subtle contact of each foot earthing itself on the decking, the tiny, dust-coloured spiders darting between the slats, the sun's benevolent embrace of my body, shadows of clouds dancing over the adjacent grassy meadow, the immaculate spontaneity of birdsong. Such was the lack of a solid sense of 'me' that the very breeze seemed to blow through my bones. The sensory world became disappearing streaks in space and collages of mental impressions running on self-propelled loops. Alive and at peace like never before, I felt a powerful union with all things. Presence was mine. The notion ran through my mind that I was on the cusp of some deep and profound insight. Then a bumblebee flew into the back of my head.

Given my acute sensitivity at the time, for a split second I thought I'd been shot. Thrown gracelessly back into mundane reality, I spun around like a startled cat, scouring the environment for danger, my mind captivated by possible threat. Then I saw the bee, having bounced off my head, merrily buzzing its haphazard course across the meadow, taking with it my refined state, which had evaporated in a trice. It was back to being wary little 'me' astride some planks of wood, self-consciously scratching my head. I was obliged to concede that if a glancing knock from a harmless insect could toss me into full egocentricity in a nanosecond, then enlightenment was some way off. How much easier it is to rebound into the anxious habits of a lifetime than to awaken fearlessly to the actuality of all things. Once again, I knew where I stood. The path of mindfulness is a great leveller.

INTIMACY WITHOUT IDENTITY

The heart of human anxiety and the wonder of mindful enquiry meet deep in the curious realm of the self. Who is it that gets anxious? What is the nature of 'me'? Meditation probes these questions, revealing something of the perpetual flux of time, space and form we call 'reality' and the way our minds embroider an identity out of it.

Mindfulness is about 'being with' whatever shows up, with clarity and acceptance. Its practice exposes a habitual preoccupation with 'I' and 'me' – that elusive sense of an enduring, unchanging self. To be a fixed and solid entity is such a pervasive (and comforting) notion that we rarely question it. But it crumbles to dust when we meditate. The nature of the self is exposed for what it is – an impermanent energy form claiming ownership over the multiple, changing aspects of existence. The meditator directly observes this process of identification – how the self is something that is being created and recreated, from one moment to the next.

If the self can be observed, then who is doing the observing? Welcome to the puzzling and multifaceted nature of identity. Because such questions tend to produce fruitless thinking, mindfulness practice favours experiential curiosity over philosophical pondering. Meditative enquiry *shows* me that I do not own awareness; it is awareness that owns me. If it were the other way around, I would do everything I could to leave out what I didn't like! In meditation, the rigorous deconstruction of psycho-physical experience reveals how the sense of 'I' is conditioned by deep-seated tendencies of liking and not liking. The self is part of a process; it is not an independent entity. It is enormously freeing to see this and to let go of a lifetime's habit of viewing thoughts, feelings and physical sensations as personal attributes.

Taking a Mindful Selfie

The calm, deep waters of mindfulness practice afford me clear glimpses of the strange and fascinating creature called self. Self is innately connected to mental grasping – it is caught up in a campaign of wanting and not wanting with the world, determined to achieve lasting comfort through its endless machinations. The self treats life like a game of Monopoly. It will buy, sell, manipulate, befriend, obstruct... do anything, in fact, for personal gain. It seeks power and security, regardless of the consequences. More than anything, the self seeks control, even presumes it. But because it has no control – the body senses, the heart emotes, the mind thinks, whether 'I' want them to or not – the self is inherently anxious. Even the presenting moment is troubling to it because the self is dependent on the *next* moment for its existence.

In my meditation practice, often the first clue that 'selfing' is happening comes through spotting mental flights of fancy where 'I' am fulfilling some ambition, manifesting some desirable quality or appearing heroic in the eyes of imagined others. Self is a compulsive fantasist, always wanting to come out on top. Similarly, when my mind is caught up in mental stories about avoiding failure, humiliation or danger, the self will be found, desperately seeking to preserve itself. The self knows how to make itself comfortable through thought! It wants to be happy. Unfortunately, it never can be. Through mindfulness, its empty, impermanent nature is revealed and its ensnaring and binding effects are felt. The illusion of things happening to a static 'me' is smashed. This paves the way for a bona fide immersion in the primary rhythms of life – unbound, ever-changing, anxiety-free.

Filling in the Background

Seeing the absence of a substantial self is different to believing there is no self at all. Of course there is a self, in the sense that you have the experience of being a person. The narrative of your life has a unique and continuous thread running through it. There may be no unchanging self behind it all but,

conventionally speaking, 'you' exist all right. Mindfulness prioritizes awareness of immediate experience, but it need not discount the benefits of mining the content of your life story in the service of a saner life. It is within past experience that you find the roots of issues that remain unresolved today. Working through the unfinished business of the past is liberating.

I have learned a lot about my anxious tendencies through such inner work. As a child growing up during the 'Troubles' in Northern Ireland, I knew about the violence and sectarian conflict surrounding me. But because I had no direct encounters with bombs or bullets, I presumed, long into adulthood, that my family's accepted version of events – a story about the Troubles being 'no big deal' and us never being in harm's way – was an accurate one. Only through psychotherapeutic work did I understand the degree to which this story denied the effects of living in a war zone and took no account of a deep disquietude I felt as a result (and have observed in others who lived during this period). My work felt like doing mental archaeology – unearthing and piecing together fragments from the past in order to build a true picture of what went before, so that I might lay it to rest.

I choose to walk a path of peace that is deeper and more durable than the excavated roots of my anxious past

Peace by Peace

What emerged was an unconscious knowing of a world traumatized by violence, engulfed in hatred and recrimination,
kept afloat with humour and alcohol. It was a place of warring
tribes and obtuse, dogmatic chieftains, bound together by traditions of battling and mutual fears of being overrun. Territory
was divided, literally, into 'safe' and 'unsafe'. Civil life was
confined by borders and boundaries where, as the poet
Seamus Heaney put it, 'my land marches your land'.[30] You
were obliged to know where you stood and where you ought
not to stand. This was a society of splits – psychic, cultural,
religious and political. Primal reactions of flight, fight and
freeze were the currency of movement. From my safe seat in
the therapy room, I recalled how the air would hang thick
with tension and fear always went unspoken.

Gradually I understood the degree to which my childhood
world had been unfathomable to me at the time. But in the
roots of my being, I knew it well – the threat of bombardment, the rationing of spontaneity, the toxic lack of trust.
Bringing all this into conscious awareness allowed me to let
go. Now I am more able to exit my internalized war zone. The
world of my childhood continues to fascinate and repel me in
equal measure. I see how anxiety runs through ancestral lines
like water and how, under a rough crust of collective ill will,
there lies an ocean of tears. When I visit childhood places,
where the air still hangs thick with tension, I relate to them

MEDITATION

WHO IS THINKING?

❋

● Sit in a comfortable, upright position and settle the body. Take a few deep breaths to aid relaxation and then let the breath return to its natural rhythm. Now purposefully direct your attention to the sensations of breathing in the body. Let the breath be your gateway and your anchor to the present moment.

● Gently and repeatedly 'point' the attention at the breath. Feel the sensations of in-breath and out-breath. When the attention wanders, patiently escort it back to the breath and start again. Relax into the simplicity of this practice.

● Now allow the attention to open up to what is happening in the mind.

● When thoughts appear, note them and intentionally pose the question: 'Who is thinking?' Notice the effect of this question on the mind. Does the mind become busy, seeking answers to its own question? Does the mind go into doubt, confusion, astonishment or surprise? Does the mind fall quiet?

● As thoughts appear, keep lightly dropping the question into the mind: 'Who is thinking?' Notice how thoughts might turn upon themselves, looking for an identity, searching for a sense of 'I' or 'me'. If the mind throws up answers, observe these as more thoughts.

● If 'you' notice you have got lost in thinking about thinking, deliberately redirect your attention to the sensations of breathing in the body. Relax. Notice one or two breaths in order to anchor the attention, then again open up to this enquiry into the nature of self.

differently. I am no longer bound by old fears. I am no longer powerless. I choose to walk a path of peace that is deeper and more durable than the excavated roots of my anxious past.

THE REVOLUTION OF EVERYDAY LIFE

◆

I like to jog on the tree-lined path that encircles my local park. Around and around I go. The same journey is different every time I make it. When I feel awake and bright, I run with a spring in my step and a sense of connection to what is happening around me. When I feel dull or out of sorts, I get preoccupied with my own exertions and things seem disjointed.

RUNNING IS MY WORKING METAPHOR FOR LIVING. How easy it is to slide into states of internal resistance and to huff and puff at displeasing conditions. This is a gateway to petty self-absorption and a breeding ground for anxiety. By contrast, mindfulness in daily life is about being alert and receptive – alive through the senses – to what is showing up. When I run unhindered by selfish concerns, open to my experience, in contact with each step, mindfulness is strong. At such times, I am aware of others around me – passers-by, playing children, dogs, birds – and am available to the spontaneous unfolding of life in the park. Mind and world interpenetrate. I become part of a living, breathing, public space. Afflictive emotions have no footing.

Being in the World

Relocating to the present moment is more than a private affair. It is a cue for – to use the words of the Stoic philosopher Seneca (1 BCE–65 CE) – 'plunging oneself into the totality of the world'.[31] Mindfulness proclaims a fearless presence in a selfless world. It is a path of action, cultivated through wisdom and compassion. Humility and wise reflection are its guides. Its path encompasses everything – what we value, how we move, the way we think, what we say, where we work, how we use the resources of our planet... The entire architecture of our life is worthy of attention. Every choice we make changes the world.

Mindfulness proclaims a fearless presence in a selfless world. It is a path of action, cultivated through wisdom and compassion

With eyes open, we discern how the joy of others is inseparable from our own and, indeed, how our own anxiety is part of a wider matrix of suffering. Mindful enquiry not only punctures the façades of substance and continuity in this phenomenal world – it alters the way we relate to its material structures. The jigsaw pieces of 'inner' and 'outer' begin to interlock. We see how the seeds of anxiety are embedded in institutions that provoke fear, stress, economic dysfunction and environmental destruction. When we no longer fall prey to fantasies of happiness residing

Hidden in my wilderness

an ancient way

beside a tinkling stream.

KEN JONES
1930–2015, ZEN POET AND TEACHER[32]

in wealth, fame and power, we are spared the cravings of materialism, which encourages us to value only what we don't yet have. Breaking out of the banal echo chambers of manufactured dreams is life-affirming. It allows us to embrace our own and others' humanity. We meet the world anew.

The power of mindfulness touches our deepest being and radiates far into the world. It reveals that peace and happiness lie within us and in between us, not outside of us. It reminds us that the world is an anxious place with much to teach us. To recover from anxiety would be like recovering from being human. Anxiety is part of the fabric of existence – it is something we must tenderly work with in order to live well. Life is a non-stop flow of appearances rolling towards us and rearing up inside us. Can we lean into it, open up to it and see what happens? Can we find pockets of space to root and grow? If we can, we reclaim this amazing chance, right now, to wake up. It only takes a moment.

ENDNOTES

◆

1. *Gestalt Therapy Verbatim* by Frederick Perls, p3 (Real People Press, Moab, UT, 1969)

2. *Gestalt Therapy: Excitement and Growth in the Human Personality* by Paul Goodman, Ralph Hefferline and Frederick Perls (Penguin, London, 1972/1951)

3. *The Nicomachean Ethics* by Aristotle, trans. T. Irwin, 'Book III' (Hackett, USA, 1999)

4. *The Anatomy of Melancholy* by Robert Burton, 'The First Partition' (New York Review of Books, New York, 2001)

5. 'In Tenebris II', *The Collected Poems of Thomas Hardy*, p151 (Wordsworth Editions Ltd, Ware, UK, 1994)

6. By Clarissa Pinkola Estés. Online at http://www.huna.org/html/cpestes.html or http://www.awakin.org/read/view.php?tid=548

7. 'The Discourse on Two Kinds of Thought', *Majjhima Nikaya* ('Middle Length Discourses'), discourse 19, Pali Canon

8. *Mindfulness-Based Cognitive Therapy for Depression* by Zindel Segal, Mark Williams and John Teasdale, p70-2 (Guilford Press, New York, 2002)

9. *Mindfulness-Based Cognitive Therapy for Depression* by Zindel Segal, Mark Williams and John Teasdale, p73-4 (Guilford Press, New York, 2002)

10. *A Blue Fire* by James Hillman, p117 (HarperPerennial, USA, 1991)

11. *There Is Nothing Wrong With You* by Cheri Huber, p184 (Keep It Simple, USA, 1993)

12. *The Girl in the Picture* by Denise Chong, p364 (Simon and Schuster, London, 2000)

13. 'Living Life No Matter What' by Tara Brach (2012). Online at http://blog.tarabrach.com/2012_08_01_archive.html

14. *Ways of Seeing* by John Berger, p9 (Penguin, London, 1972)

15. *Creative Process in Gestalt Therapy* by Joseph Zinker, p32 (Vintage, USA, 1978)

16. Various discourses, *Sutta-pitaka* ('Basket of Discourses'), Pali Canon

17. 'Guarding', *Anguttara Nikaya* ('Numerical Discourses'), Book of Fours discourse 117, Pali Canon

18. 'Alchemical Studies' (Vol. 13), *The Collected Works of C.G. Jung* by Carl Jung, trans. R.F.C. Hull, p265 (Bollingen Series XX/Princeton University Press, New Jersey, 1970)

19. *The Complete Poetical Works and Letters of John Keats* (Cambridge Edition), p277 (Houghton Mifflin Co., New York, 1899)

20. Quoted in *Tales From The Tao* by S. Towler and J. Cleare, p66 (Watkins, London, 2005)

21. 'The Privatisation of Spirituality. Genetically Modified Practice for Business: A Critique' by Christopher Titmuss (2014). Online at http://christophertitmuss.org/blog/the-privatisation-of-spirituality-genetically-modified-practice-for-business

22. 'Beyond McMindfulness' by Ron Purser and David Loy (2013). Online at http://www.huffingtonpost.com/ron-purser/beyond-mcmindfulness_b_3519289.html

23. *The Concept of Anxiety* by Søren Kierkegaard, trans. R. Thomte and A. B. Anderson (Princeton University Press, New Jersey, 1980)

24. *Being and Time* by Martin Heidegger, trans. J. McQuarrie and E. Robinson (Blackwell, Oxford, 2005)

25. *The Concept of Anxiety* by Søren Kierkegaard, trans. R. Thomte and A. B. Anderson, p61 (Princeton University Press, New Jersey, 1980)

26. Various discourses, *Sutta-pitaka* ('Basket of Discourses'), Pali Canon

27. 'Welcoming Death' by Bhante Bodhidhamma. Online at http://www.satipanya.org.uk/index.php?page=tip

28. Quoted in *Seeking the Heart of Wisdom* by J. Goldstein and J. Kornfield, p6 (Shambhala, Boston, 1987)

29. *Dhammpada* ('Verses on the Eternal Truth'), verse 95, Pali Canon

30. *Something to Write Home About: Seamus Heaney*, directed by David Hammond (BBC TV Northern Ireland, 1998).

31. Quoted in *Philosophy as a Way of Life* by Pierre Hadot, p208 (Blackwell, Oxford, 1995)

32. *Bog Cotton: Haiku Stories and Haiku* by Ken Jones, p94 (Alba Publishing, Uxbridge, UK, 2012). Reproduced with permission.

INDEX

DEDICATION

For my family

ACKNOWLEDGEMENTS

Many people – teachers, friends, colleagues and clients – have indirectly contributed to this book. In particular, I wish to acknowledge the debt I owe to Bhante Bodhidhamma of Satipanya Buddhist Retreat, teachers from the Theravada Forest Sangha and senior teachers within the Western insight meditation tradition.

I am grateful to Peter Harvey for his astute guidance in the study of Buddhism, Jon Kabat-Zinn for his pioneering efforts in bringing mindfulness into secular settings, and John Teasdale, Zindel Segal and Mark Williams for their work on Mindfulness-Based Cognitive Therapy.

In the psychotherapeutic world, I am indebted to the Gestalt Therapy tradition for its abiding emphasis on experiential awareness, and the Psychodynamic and Cognitive-Behavioural traditions for their insights into working skilfully with anxiety.

My gratitude to Michelle Cobbin for her boundless support and divine tolerance, and to others who, perhaps unknowingly, lent shape to this book: Anne Cole, Dheeresh Turnbull, David Glendining and Polly Irvin.

For their keen eyes and encouraging words, my heartfelt thanks to Monica Perdoni, Jenni Davis, Joanna Bentley and Susan Kelly of Ivy Press.